How to Cheer Up a Capricorn

How to Cheer Up
a Capricorn

Mary L. English

BOOKS

Winchester, UK
Washington, USA

First published by O-Books, 2011
O-Books is an imprint of John Hunt Publishing Ltd., Laurel House, Station Approach,
Alresford, Hants, SO24 9JH, UK
office1@o-books.net
www.o-books.com

For distributor details and how to order please visit the 'Ordering' section on our website.

ISBN: 978 1 84694 664 6

A CIP catalogue record for this book is available from the British Library.

Design: Lee Nash

Printed in the UK by CPI Antony Rowe
Printed in the USA by Offset Paperback Mfrs, Inc

We operate a distinctive and ethical publishing philosophy in all
areas of our business, from our global network of authors to
production and worldwide distribution.

CONTENTS

Also by Mary L English

6 Easy Steps in Astrology
The Birth Charts of Indigo Children
How to Survive a Pisces (O-Books)
How to Bond with an Aquarius (O-Books)

Please visit Mary's site at www.maryenglish.com

This book is dedicated to my youngest (best) sister:
Katherine Francis English.
May every passing day bring more happiness to you.

Acknowledgements

I would like to thank the following people:

My lovely Taurus husband who makes my life so wonderful.

My son for being the Libran that makes me always look on the other side.

Marina, a lovely Pisces who helped encourage me in the beginning.

Tony, Pat & Oksana for their welcome editing skills.

Caroline Lewis-Jones for her moral support.

Mabel, Jessica and Usha for their understanding.

Laura and Mandy for their friendship.

Mari and Alix for their superior kindness and hospitality.

Peter and Tammy Kwan for first-aid-tea and computer knowledge

Noel and Bernard for saying 'No' *so* nicely.

John my publisher for being the person that fought tooth and nail to get this book published and all the staff at O-Books including Kate, Maria, Trevor, Stuart, Lee, Mary, Elizabeth and Radley.

And last but not least my lovely clients for their valued contributions.

Introduction

Why the title of this book?

After the publication of How to Survive a Pisces, I was asked by my clients if I was going to write about their sign, so I embarked on writing about each sign of the Zodiac. As I'd started with my own sign, Pisces, the last sign, I thought I'd go backwards through the Zodiac. Why not?

As much as I respect other Sun sign authors, Linda Goodman included, I thought I'd go backwards as I wanted to work slowly because if I started with Aries (which was Linda's sign), and is such a busy, fast sign, I might rush and then get tired and not finish.

So, I started with the signs closest to my sign, my second book being How to Bond with an Aquarius as my mother, 2 sisters, ex mother-in-law and now sadly deceased Auntie are of that independent sign. And as I'd promised myself to go backwards, it then meant I had to write about Capricorn next.

This wasn't an easy option.

Even though I have a sister who is Capricorn, a dear Homeopathic friend (whose husband is also Capricorn) and two second-cousins, the more I thought about, or read about Capricorns, the more it seemed it would be an uphill struggle.

My grandmother also was a Capricorn and her husband (my grandfather) died early aged 60 of TB. She spent the next 34 years widowed but very independent. My memory of her was that she was very opinionated and either loved you, or not. There was no in between. I never knew what her first name was. We only knew her as 'Grandma English'

My mother wrote about in her book *Branching Out Fruits of the Tree*:

Ena, as she was known in the family, was made of sterner stuff than her husband Reginald and she lived on until the ripe old age of 94.

All her life, which had not been easy, she remained a staunch Catholic. She never lowered their standards and she either loved or hated and certainly never forgave her enemies but was generous to those she loved – luckily I was one of those.

I then had to think of a title, one that would inspire others to learn about this sign, but also to help those that struggle with the sign themselves. I wasn't going to write just about the fun side of the sign; I needed to write about their Achilles heel. The thing that other people think they struggle with, which I found is 'being happy'.

And to make the writing of this book more meaningful, just as I got to the last chapter and was 'tidying-things-up', I suffered an unexpected and humungous computer crash which effectively wiped-away 50% of this book... and turned it into hieroglyphics. No amount of software fixes would recreate 4 months of work and over 12,000 words and I was left with the sorry task of having to rewrite the last 3 chapters. The only people who truly knew how I felt were other authors, of which my older sister Lucy is one, and after spending the weekend weeping and cursing Jupiter and Uranus retrograde, her sympathetic ear and reminder to 'back-up EVERYWHERE' brought me some solace and I carried on... even though I felt very UN-happy.

It was during this sad episode that I realised I had to call upon my own Saturn (which you will learn about soon) which is luckily in Capricorn, so I could: 'grit teeth, nose to the grindstone, no use making a fuss, get on with it', otherwise you wouldn't be reading this book at all. It also gave me some understanding of Capricorn's need to succeed, and get the job done, regardless of outside occurrences.

Being Glum
As my job is as an Astrologer (and Homeopath), I spend a lot of my time helping people with their relationships and one of the

things that my clients mostly say about Capricorns is: 'They always seem to be so unhappy.' Now, this varies from complete manic depression, to being glum and unexcited and most of the complaints come from the Fire signs: Aries, Leo and Sagittarius.

The Air signs complain a little too, but they don't generally hang around much with Capricorns anyway... So I thought I'd investigate exactly why Capricorns can seem so unhappy and I spoke to various Capricorns, asked their opinions, spoke to partners of Capricorns and researched famous... and not so famous men and woman of December to January birth. It was a very enlightening experience and I hope in the pages of this little book that I will dispel some of the myths of Capricorn, because if we were to believe every word written about Capricorn we'd become very gloomy indeed. I'd also like to illustrate their good points and assist you in understanding what motivates them and if you're in a stuck place, how to cheer them up. I will also give you some guidance on ways to tackle the Capricorns you know depending on what sign you are.

Happiness and Gloom

I must admit that writing this book was a bit of a challenge. Understanding the motivations of the Capricorn ideal involved lengthy thought about the nature of happiness... and gloom, because Capricorn is famed for its ability to be serious.

My first port of call was to ask a creative Capricorn writer and poet what made him happy.

James was born in Liverpool to a surgeon father and teacher mother. He was the only boy of four children and second born. He was much later to discover that he was the only child his parents had actually planned for. During his childhood his father was relatively absent working long hours, so he grew up in a predominantly female household with a sort of shadowy, distant but powerful father figure.

He failed to get into the grammar school his parents had

ambitions for, so ended up in a comprehensive where many of the other pupils thought he was posh because of his lack of local accent. There was some bullying. He didn't achieve the exam results his parents wanted him to, in order to go into medicine, as his skills were more geared towards the arts and creativity. His father died suddenly of a heart attack when James was 17. He went away one weekend, hill climbing, and collapsed and died on Ben Nevis.

At 18 James gained a place at a school of art and went there to study fine art, specialising in sculpture. This was both a thrilling and difficult time as he didn't feel as prepared for the away-from-home art school life as many of his peers, but he managed to make several good friends and gained a degree. During his time at college, his mother became an alcoholic and spent some time in a drying-out clinic.

He then moved to London and spent many years unemployed and stoned. He dabbled in arts and crafts, primarily ceramics, eventually securing a studio to work from, but never really earning a living from his creativity. However, he didn't want to give it up for a 'proper job' and so attended numerous courses aimed at the unemployed and became self-employed for short periods. He spent a year or so during this period working as a hospital porter, but gave that up as soon as his debts were paid. One night he went to an open mic and decided he would try and read out some of his own poetry. He enjoyed it, and after a few years became the organiser and host of the night, which lead to organising other events. He met many new friends there, which he still has today.

"James," I said, "I'd like to ask a quick question. What makes you happy?"

What made me chuckle was how he 'had to come back' to me on that:

"Hi Mary, will answer your questions this evening, hopefully. But still trying to define 'happy'."

Glorious! He just couldn't answer the question until he had defined happiness.

Five hours later, he came back with a reply:

What makes me happy?
Being absorbed in an activity (usually artistic/creative).

Being absorbed in a positive experience (walking, making, talking etc). Experiencing positive reactions to the results of work (entertaining an audience or people admiring my visual art).

Seeing other people benefit from my efforts (if running a workshop or organizing an event – being able to watch an audience or learners experience the same thrill I have from similar situations in the past). Lack of worry/anxiety – usually when 'living in the moment' either through the above, or in some way being distracted from the cares and woes of life, i.e. by company, situation or inebriation!

Security.
Freedom.

"How do you know you're happy?" I asked.

Usually in retrospect. Although I am training myself to appreciate happy times by internally stepping back and reviewing my emotional state. I have sometimes felt a feeling of what I call 'invulnerability', where whatever someone says or does will not upset me and I view the world with a mild amount of amusement at its bizarreness.

That may be happiness.

I spend a lot of time inside my own head, often working through and replaying situations and seeking solutions to perceived problems. When I am not doing this, I think I am happier. (Although the process of solving artistic/creative problems is often a very pleasurable experience.) Sometimes if I find myself singing to myself or dancing about a bit to myself, I realise I must be happy; sometimes that's excitement (sometimes with no real reason to be excited).

This is an interesting question. I don't think of myself as a happy person (should that be 'a cheerful person'?), and people often think I am unhappy because I do not smile easily and can take things too seriously. I'm not one of those people who can say things like 'The colour green makes me happy,' or 'My dog makes me happy.' I believe that happiness is a by-product of situation and can often only be recognised in retrospect. Possibly.

Is pragmatism a Capricornian trait?

Yes, pragmatism is a trait of all Capricorns. We will find out more about that in a minute....

I then asked another Capricorn the same question.

Rachel lives in the city with her husband and young daughter and works for a local Steiner School as a part-time teacher. First she describes what her Capricorn grandmother used to say to her:

My Granny used to mention 'us hardworking Capricorns'. She was a lovely funny loving lady who looked after her family of 12 siblings when her mother died in her early 40's due to a burst appendix.

"What makes you happy, Rachel?" I asked.

Sorority,* although not always the case for me, spending time with family (I can feel more frustration to be honest) – but it was definitely the case for my Capricorn granny (mentioned before) – happiness being with her family around her, but then two of her babies died about one year old and she had to run through bombed streets during the war carrying her other baby and toddler through the blitzes. I think she never took 'happiness for granted', she delighted in happy times and conviviality and retelling hilarious memories, laughing helplessly until tears rolled down her face from laughter.

My cousin who is a Capricorn takes great delight in funny

things the kids say (she never boasts about her children's 'achieve-ments') but she always has a bunch of funny stories about things they've said, a bit self-deprecating, always hilarious.
*devotional sisterhood

I then asked another Capricorn, Lisa, what made her happy and how did she know when she's happy.

Here is her reply:

Experiencing inspiration, particularly from the natural world (from a fleeting effect of light to the majesty of mountains); challenging myself and succeeding in that challenge. I know when I'm happy, possibly unusually for a Capricorn, as I am either high (normal state of affairs, certainly through my 40's!) or low (relatively rare) – I'm rarely anywhere in the middle. I would say that when truly happy I feel an overwhelming sense of well-being.

I then asked one final question: "On a scale of 1–10 (10 being high, 1 being low), how pragmatic are you?

"*8,*" was her reply...

So here we have 'from the horse's mouth' three examples of what makes a Capricorn happy... now that's not quite the same as cheering one up. That will be discussed later.

First of all we need to understand a little about Astrology, where it came from and where it is now, so we can accurately assess, in an Astrological manner, what sort of Capricorn we are dating, mothering, fathering or working with.

For a fuller account of the history of Astrology, please see my first book *How To Survive a Pisces* or Nick Campion's detailed account of Astrology's beginnings in his 2 volumes: *The Dawn of Astrology* and *The Golden Age of Astrology*:

Astrology is not a single practice or idea; it includes multiple narratives about the nature of the world. If we examine its history carefully we can see that it is variously, a form of magic, a system of prediction, a model for psychological growth, a science, a spiritual tool, a religion and a system of divination, definitions which are not mutually exclusive.[1]

Or as Franz Cumont says in *Astrology and Religion Among the Greeks and Romans*:

Astrology is an English translation of a Latin translation of a Greek translation of a Babylonian nomenclature.*
*a system of names assigned to objects or items in a particular science or art.

We know full well that what the Babylonians saw as planets travelling through constellations in the sky is now the sky divided into 12 equal parts and each 'part' is a sign of the Zodiac, the first 'part' being Aries. We no longer use the constellations in the sky named after certain Gods and remembered today as the various Sun signs such as Gemini. No, today our Astrology is calculated from the spring solstice: Aries, to the Autumn Solstice: Libra and all the others are parts of the sky divided equally into the other 10 signs. A bit like the periodic table. The different lines and levels of it don't actually exist; they are just a way of recording the atomic weights of each element in nature. It's a 'work-in-progress'. Astrology is the same. It isn't finite and we discover new things all the time.

The movements of the planets going through each sign of the Zodiac are recorded in a publication called an 'Ephemeris'. That's where the maths takes place, which is why calculating a Horoscope or Birth Chart is so much easier now. Computers have speeded up the ability to refine the information. And just for the record, the Moon and the Sun are not planets.

Planet: A celestial body that orbits around the Sun.

Star: With the exception of the Moon and the planets, every fixed point of light in the sky is a star, including the Sun.

In Astrology we use the term 'planet' for all the bits we use. So if you catch me calling the Sun a planet, that is an Astrological term, not one used in astronomy.

There are two types of Astrology practiced in the west. Tropical Astrology which gives the position of a planet by sign, and Sidereal which gives the position by constellation. Over 4,000 years ago, on the vernal equinox, the first day of Spring, the Sun was in the constellation of Aries. Now because of the Earth wobbling on its axis and a thing called 'precession', the Sun enters in the sign of Aries but in the constellation of Pisces. I practice Tropical Astrology, taking into account that as far as the planets are today, they've shifted. Both systems have value, there is no 'right' or 'wrong'; I just prefer the older one.

With there being 10 'planets' that we take into account in a chart, making an accurate summary of its potential can be daunting for a newbie, so for the purposes of this book and for simplicity's sake, all we will be concentrating on are 3 important things: the Ascendant – the 'time' of birth; the 'house' the Sun is in; and the sign of the Moon.

I look at Astrology as being a nifty way to understand people, and if we can understand each other, the world is a friendlier place. So let us find out about the sign we're going to help 'Cheer Up'.

Chapter 1

The Sign:
Serious, Responsible, Stoic, Pragmatic

To find out if someone is truly a Capricorn, you will need to use a good computer program or ask an Astrologer. For the purposes of this book, all *you* will need is one good website, which Astrologers use, called www.astro.com.

The dates that are Capricorn are *generally* from the 22nd December to the 20th January. This is when the Sun goes through the part of the sky Astrologers have named Capricorn. However, these dates can vary as the Sun doesn't move at the same rate as the days in the month, as we have some months with only 30 days and they vary from year to year and they also vary depending on where your Capricorn was born.

You will get a different result from being born in Australia to being born in Germany, so check with that good website and make sure your Capricorn is a Capricorn because if they were born early on the morning of the 22nd December 1979 and born in London at 2am, they'd be a Sagittarius, and if they were born at 6pm on the same date in Berlin in Germany, they'd be a Capricorn.

Remember, please double-check your dates and times.

A.A.A. = Accuracy Aids Adaptation.

So, you now know you've got a Capricorn in your life. What is a Capricorn?

What words do we use to describe this unusual species?

I thought for the purposes of balance (I have Sun in the 7th house) that I'd consult some Astrological reference books to see what words have been used in the past.

Let's go back in time and ask Colin Evans editor of *The New Waite's Compendium of Natal Astrology*, 1971 and see what he says:

"Capricorn individuals are economical, practical, persevering, shrewd, diplomatic, reserved and cautious."[3]

Crikey! They are really serious sounding words, aren't they? Are all Capricorns like this?

Let's ask someone else. Here's Terry Dwyer, author of *How to Write an Astrological Synthesis*, 1985:

"Disciplined, stern, conventional, narrow-minded, serious, pessimistic, careful, calculating, prudent, mean, ambitious, and callous."[4]

Hmm, this doesn't sound much better does it? Would you want to be described like this? Is this description true?

Let's ask a few women. Here are Mary Coleman's thoughts from *Picking Your Perfect Partner Through Astrology* in 1996:

"Provident, businesslike, introverted, prestige-orientated and practical... resourceful, self-disciplined and obedient... severe, conservative and lacking spontaneity."[5]

Mmm this sounds like a tax man, are these people human?

Let's ask Linda Goodman, that wonderful Astrologer who influenced a whole three generations of Astrology-liking people:

"There's always a faint aura of melancholy and seriousness surrounding the Saturn personality."[6]

Not as bad, but still a bit on the negative side.

Now let's ask what Maritha Pottenger thinks about people with Sun in Capricorn. Her key words are:

"Responsibility, Tradition, Authority, Career."[7]

There certainly seems to be some repeating words here.

Let's turn to Donna Cunningham in 1999:

"People with Capricorn Suns need success for their self-worth and for the parental approval their self-worth requires."[8]

And last but not least, Marion D. March and Joan McEvers in *The Only Way To Learn Astrology* use the words:

"Cautious, responsible, scrupulous, conventional, businesslike, perfectionist, practical, hardworking, economical, serious (that word again), egotistic, domineering, fatalistic, stubborn, brooding, inhibited and status-seeking."[9]

OK, I think you get the drift now. Capricorns are hard-headed, career-orientated, serious loners... wherever did these ideas come from?

Is this all true?

Well, like everything in life, some things are true and some things are either exaggeration or a complete pack of lies... but whichever way you look at it, your average Capricorn *isn't* running around in a tutu, wearing pink fluffy dresses and worrying about their lipstick.

Not even Kate Moss... they are private individuals:

"Thank you for the interest in Kate and for your email. Kate's a very private individual and we cannot give you the details you have requested. Apologies, but we never discuss her private life."

All I'd asked for was her birth time, so I could make her correct Birth Chart. I wasn't asking about her bank balance or who she was dating. Sigh. I suppose that's also because she has a Scorpio Moon but we'll come to Moons in a minute.

After some analysis and from talking to as many Capricorn

clients and relatives of Capricorns as I could, I decided that the best words to describe a Capricorn would be: Serious, Responsible, Stoic and Pragmatic.

Serious

The *Oxford Dictionary of Current English* defines serious as:

"thoughtful, earnest, demanding thought, sincere, not (merely) frivolous."

Love the last bit: 'not' frivolous, that would certainly be a phrase I'd use to describe a Capricorn!

If we go a little way past Astrology and see what a Capricorn author has (unknowingly) written about themselves and their sign we'll see that the above descriptions aren't so far off the mark.

When he [Christopher Robin] was three, we took a house in North Wales for August with the Nigel Playfairs. It rained continuously... In a week I was screaming with agoraphobia. Somehow I must escape. I pleaded urgent inspiration, took a pencil and an exercise-book and escaped to the summer-house. It contained a chair and a table. I sat down on the chair, put my exercise-book on the table, and gazed ecstatically at a wall of mist which might have been hiding Snowdon or the Serpentine for all I saw or cared. I was alone... So there I was with an exercise- book and a pencil, and a fixed determination not to leave the heavenly solitude of that summer-house until it stopped raining and there in London were two people telling me what to write and there on the other side of the lawn was a child with whom I had lived for three years... and here within me were unforgettable memories of my own childhood... what was I writing? A child's book of verses obviously.

Not a whole book, of course; but to write a few would be fun – until I was tired of it. Besides, my pencil had an india-rubber at the back; just the thing for poetry. I had eleven wet days in that summer-house and wrote eleven sets of verses. Then we went back to London.

A little apologetically: feeling that this wasn't really work: feeling that a man of stronger character would be writing that detective-story and making £2,000 for the family: a little as if I were slipping off to Lord's in the morning, or lying in a deck-chair at Osborne reading a novel, I went on writing verses. By the end of the year I had written enough for a book.[10]

In this fantastic little excerpt A.A. Milne, who was a Capricorn, can't even *think* that he should be making money doing something he enjoys. He thinks it is like 'slipping off to Lord's' or 'lying in a deck-chair' when a 'stronger' character would be writing something (key Capricorn-word-alert) 'serious' like a detective novel.

You can also see A.A. Milne's character slipping through his other writing.

With the character Eeyore out of Winnie the Pooh we have him saying things like:

"Is anything the matter? You seem so sad, Eeyore."

"Sad? Why shouldn't I be sad? It's my birthday. The happiest day of the year."

"Your birthday?" said Pooh in great surprise.

"Of course it is. Can't you see? Look at all the presents I have had."

He waved a foot from side to side. "Look at the birthday cake. Candles and pink sugar."

Pooh looked – first to the right and then to the left. "Presents?" said Pooh. "Birthday cake?" said Pooh. "Where?"

"Can't you see them?"

"No," said Pooh.

"Neither can I," said Eeyore. "Joke," he explained. "Ha ha!"

Pooh scratched his head, being a little puzzled by all this.

"But is it really your birthday?" he asked.

"It is."

"Oh! Well, many happy returns of the day, Eeyore."

"And many happy returns to you, Pooh Bear."

"But it isn't my birthday."

"No, it's mine."

"But you said, 'Many happy returns' –"

"Well, why not? You don't always want to be miserable on my birthday, do you?"

"Oh, I see," said Pooh.

"It's bad enough," said Eeyore, almost breaking down, "being miserable myself, what with no present and no cake and no candles, and no proper notice taken of me at all, but if everyone else is going to be miserable too – "[11]

I have a theory that you can only write about things well, that you have experienced yourself and I think Eeyore is a part of A.A. Milne. Could he be his inner-self?

Is that why he could describe so well how 'he' might feel if 'his' birthday was forgotten? Could this be a Capricorn way of dealing with the emotion of their birthday not being remembered?

He's distraught that none of his friends have remembered his birthday, no cakes, no candles and instead of jumping up and down making a fuss, he's being sarcastic, hurt and difficult.

Not that other signs wouldn't *feel* the same, but a Capricorn won't 'do' anything when their pride has been hurt or they've been snubbed. They just sort of shrug and use it as evidence that the world can an unhelpful place at times.

Here we have a 'modern-day' Capricorn talking about her sign.

Amanda has recently retired from her responsible job in the health service. She now lives on her own and spends her time in creative pursuits:

I do think I am Capricornus through and through; although there remains that niggling little objection some people express as to the 'suspicious compatibility' of the zodiac signs to everyone – do people subconsciously want to reflect the positive aspects of their individual signs, for example? I don't think so. There would seem to be far too many coincidences in life for this to be true, if coincidences even exist, that is... Anyway; personally I am a reserved person (with impeccable manners, teehee!) and act rather too cautious for my own good. I do indeed have ambitious career goals, yet in no way am I a girl, star-struck by foolish hopes and dreams; to which belies one of my more negative assets – I'm a bit pessimistic at times, which in itself can lead to trouble all on its own, believe me— I blame my perfectionist streak. My best friend is Cancerian – it then truly came as no surprise to me when I discovered our signs are very compatible with each other indeed. And whilst regarding friends – well, I'll admit it's hard sometimes for me to socialise since I am rather shy (not after a bottle of rosé though – gasp!), but at least my friends find my sense of humor amusing, particularly my famous (or should I say infamous?) one-liners! So there we go. I read this quote about Capricorns on an Astrology website recently: "They are voices of reason in a chaotic world." I would definitely hope so!

Amanda freely admits to 'being cautious' and I loved the bit about not being 'star-struck by foolish hopes and dreams'.

So file away in the back of your mind the word serious, because it will make more sense when you learn about other the Capricorn qualities.

Responsible

'Morally accountable for actions' is how my *Oxford English Dictionary* describes the word responsible. So in the light of this view let's look at how Capricorns actually cope with responsibility.

From my own personal observations, Capricorns like to have

a certain amount of responsibility. They like to feel that they are directing or overseeing or taking part in something 'important' depending on where the importance lies.

You must also take into account that the clients I see in my private practice are unhappy. They don't phone me up for an appointment when they're just won the lottery, they ring me because 'something has happened' and they need some help/guidance/support to sort it out.

Funnily enough, while I was writing this book I happened to have more than my usual intake of Capricorn clients, which was very useful for writing purposes. One was going through a divorce and needed to 'sort-out' the finances; another was worried about her son as she felt they had fallen-out but wasn't sure why. Another was very ill and wasn't getting any relief from the medical profession and needed me to help him get the diagnosis he needed, so he could get the right treatment.

All of these clients came to see me, not the minute something had happened (unlike a Fire sign, they get on the phone as it's happening!), but after a long amount of struggle and sorrow related to the problems. Their 'status' and position of responsibility had altered and they wanted to get back to exactly where they were before it all-went-wrong.

So what sort of responsibilities do Capricorns enjoy?

First of all I don't think we should use the word enjoy. They don't enjoy responsibility, like you might 'enjoy' an ice cream, they just feel better when there is some in their life.

A Capricorn mother will feel better knowing all the effort she has put into raising her daughter will bring the results she was focused on. Like getting a good job, or going to university. Sensible forward focused results.

Things can get tricky if the child is headstrong or fluffy and doesn't want to go to university or even worse wants to join a rock band!

A Capricorn Dad might want his son to get good grades, aim

for 'A's', which again is a lovely ambition for the Capricorn, but will wreak havoc with an Aquarius or a Pisces.

So many parents live their failed ambitions through their children, which I think is an awful shame. How better it would be for them to realise their own hopes and dreams... and be happy.

Now, obviously, not everyone fails at what they do. Some people are strong enough to find their path in life and live it.

Isaac Newton and the Royal Mint

A classic Capricorn example of someone spending a lot of energy on their life-path and eventually getting there is Isaac Newton who is remembered for his discovery/understanding/explanation of gravity. But he spent the early part of his life in conditions that would throw any modern man.

His father died before he was even born, his mother remarried and he was sent to live with his grandmother. He hated his stepfather, who also died and his mother remarried again.

His mother wanted him to be a farmer. A master at his school persuaded his mother to allow him to continue his education and the rest, as they say, is history.

He joined Cambridge University aged 18 as a student where he had to 'work for his keep' and spent 35 years there studying and later lecturing. When he was 53, instead of accepting a professorship at the university he took a position at the Royal Mint in London. He actually spent over 20 years of his working life with the Royal Mint and was responsible for securing and accounting for England's repository of gold.

Now, excuse me if it sounds as if I'm trivialising his life, but 'being responsible' for the countries gold stash sounds a reasonably responsible job to me. Not one I'd want. This particular Capricorn stayed focused on his future goal, didn't let anything get in his way, steadily, and slowly over a number of years rose to a position of great responsibility.

Now, a Capricorn isn't always going to get to those sorts of heights of responsibility. They might be responsible for something far more modest, but still important, like their family, or their job, or some part of the company they work for. Whatever it may be, they will like to have that responsibility.

The clients I see are the ones who have *lost* that responsibility. They have lost their job, or sometimes even their health or their wife or their husband and that, for a Capricorn, is a heavy loss to bear.

They might be responsible for a ward in a hospital running properly. I think of the old-fashioned nursing matrons as being Capricorns. Running things in a shipshape manner. Or a designer, responsible for each issue of a magazine being correctly laid-out and containing all the relevant advertisements. Or a head gardener in a stately home, ensuring that the plants are well-tended and the staff are turned out on time, wearing their uniforms and employed productively.

A Capricorn will want to be responsible and accountable for something or someone.

Stoic

The Stoics were members of an Ancient Greek school of philosophy who thought that emotions and 'letting-it-all-hang-out' were not the best way to live happily.

'A member of an ancient Greek school of philosophy that asserted that happiness can only be achieved by accepting life's ups and downs as the products of unalterable destiny. The school was founded around 308 BC by Zeno.'

They believed in moderation.

To have feelings and thoughts but not to be ruled by them.

Now the word means: 'Showing admirable patience and endurance in the face of adversity without complaining or getting upset.'

Other words associated with Stoicism in Roget's Thesaurus are inexcitability, patience and calm.

Something that touched me while I was writing this book was the level of stoic-ness a Capricorn displays, against all the odds. Now this is different from being bloody-minded, or fixed in opinion. It's the ability to put up with stuff other people would run away from.

And why is this?

My youngest sister, who has Downs Syndrome and to whom this book is dedicated, is a Capricorn and suffered from months of unhappiness and bad health. She had to reach a very bad state of health before anyone did anything but I was amazed at her powers of stoic-ness. Even though she was in pain, when she was 'told' that she was all right, instead of arguing and making a fuss, she just started to fade away. And unlike a Fire sign, who would have been jumping around, shouting to all and sundry that they were suffering, or an Air sign who would have wanted to get medical opinions from everyone they know including the postman, or a Water sign who would have spent hours weeping and working their way through the tissues, she just carried on, repeating she was in pain... until finally she collapsed in the kitchen and was rushed to the hospital.

It took a lot of badgering and hospital visits and numerous medical hours to get her back to a better state of health. *Trust* an Earth sign when they tell you they don't feel well, and if they are a Capricorn and they say they're not feeling well, listen *very* carefully because their version of unwell might be your version of terminal.

Why do Capricorns stay in jobs or situations that would make the Air signs flee or the Fire signs want to fight back?

It comes from two places: their ruling planet Saturn, which urges them to 'do the responsible thing' and their ability to 'work towards a future goal'.

I know Capricorn women who will stay in unhappy relation-ships because they want the status that marriage brings them, and the hope that at some point in the future they can 'live their dream'. They will put up with vast amounts of suffering in the hope that things will improve and they'll get to the place of their personal expectations. Earth signs don't rush. And Capricorns are working in their heads so far into the future. It amazes me how they do it. Maybe that hope that things will get better allows them to put up with emotional stuff that would leave a Water sign gasping for air.

And Capricorns can take their time. They can come from severely disadvantaged back-grounds and get to their Nirvana by their sheer desire to reach the top of the figurative mountain.

Elvis Presley, the Man Who 'Couldn't Sing'

Elvis Presley came from a very humble beginning. His family often relied on help from neighbours and government food assistance. When he entered first grade, his instructors regarded him as 'average' and by sixth grade in September 1946, Presley was regarded 'as a loner'. Elvis received a 'C' in music in eighth grade. He was generally too shy to perform openly, and was occasionally bullied by classmates who viewed him as a 'Mama's boy'.

At 18 he cut his first record in the Sun studios and by the age of 19 he had failed an audition for a local vocal quartet. He explained to his father, "They told me I couldn't sing." He then began working as a truck driver and approached a local band to fill the position as a vocalist but they advised Presley to stick to truck driving, "because you're never going to make it as a singer."

So here we have a man who was to become one of the world's most well-known singers who was told repeatedly that what he did and who he was wasn't up to much. That man, like him or hate him, recorded over 18 No 1 albums and over 30 No 1 singles.[12]

Clients I have seen want me to understand that they have 'stood their ground' under terrible opposition or circumstances but managed to pull through. They want me to recognise that they have staying power, that they can beat the opposition by sheer force of will.

Pragmatic

Sometimes to understand a word, we have to look at other words that are associated with it. In the Thesaurus other words for pragmatic are: practical, realistic, hard-headed, sensible, matter-of-fact, no-nonsense and down-to-earth.

Aren't these all things that we have spent years saying that Capricorns are? Are they not prime examples of the qualities that Capricorns like to live their lives by?

Pragmatic is described in the Encarta Dictionary as: "more concerned with practical results than with theories and principles."

Now don't ask me where the idea that Capricorn is pragmatic came from. I'm not sure I know. I expect it's one of those meme things. Whereby if you say something enough, and it's handed-down from generation to generation, it then becomes fact. What I'm helping you understand is a little about Western Astrology and how we, in the West, use certain words and relate them to certain characteristics of each star sign.

So, pragmatic.

How pragmatic is a Capricorn?

Again it depends where their Sun is located in their chart, what sign their Moon is, and the sign of their Ascendant; but uniting the species is a need to have the practical 'things' in life organised before the fancy stuff can be considered.

If I do a reading for a Capricorn, they will want to know, before I start, exactly what I am going to 'do'. They will always want to know real, graspable, facts. It's no use me waffling on about fluffy stuff. They want to hear that they can sort out their finances, get money owed to them back, sort out divorce proceedings, sell their house, get promotion... I'm sure you get my drift. And most of the time, I won't even *see* a Capricorn in private practice until something really horrible has been happening is their lives and has done for quite a while.

McCartney Money

Let me give you a teeny example. Heather Mills is a Capricorn with Moon in Gemini. Paul McCartney her ex-husband is a Gemini with Moon in Leo. When they divorced the thing that became the most reported aspect of their divorce was the financial arrangements. She didn't just want a settlement, she wanted a specific amount. This is practical stuff.

They weren't falling out about who had the kids, or where they were going to live or who had whose name but how much the settlement would be, which ended when the judge 'awarded' Heather £24.3 million.

What else do we know about Capricorn pragmatism?

Woolly Vest and Knickers

A good friend of mine's mother was a Capricorn. She had a very good relationship with her and remembered her fondly as being practical and caring. When my friend was very young, a family moved next door to them and her mother was concerned as they were so obviously very poor. She found a knitted blanket and unpicked it, washed the wool and hung it to dry on the line and then used the wool to make underwear for the children.

Vests and knickers.

This was soon after the Second World War and rationing was still in place, so things were scarce but her mother found the time and resources to make sure someone else was better off. If 'tinkers' came round the house selling things, she'd invite them in and make them food and a cup of tea. Anyone that was worse off than herself, she found practical, sensible ways to help them.

Now most of the time, most people have the basics in life organised. They have an income, a house, maybe a partner, maybe some children and some hobbies. These are people I won't see in private practice. But when someone loses their job, gets the sack, has an affair, gets terribly ill and loses their home or even falls out with someone in their family, they will make an appointment to see me.

I don't want you getting the impression that all Capricorns are busy building large empires or are obsessed with money. They're not. What I see in private practice are clients whose worlds have fallen apart and my job is to help them get back on track. So when I say that the Capricorn clients I see are worried about their marriages and homes and incomes it's because those are things that we might take for granted, have now gone. And what I'm trying to convey is, what is important to this sign. And these are very important things to a Capricorn because they don't take them for granted.

Stable Environment

Bernie is a Capricorn who lives in the US and works with local government in a management position. She has Moon in Aquarius. When I asked her what made her happy, and when does she know when she's happy, she replied:

> I know I'm happy when I am totally in the moment and nothing else matters… my family makes me happy and seeing that everyone around me is content. I also need my ALONE time so I can get my head together… also I am happy when I have a stable environment. Job, house, car, must all be in order.

In addition to her family she needs stability with her job, house and car. Without these practical things in a Capricorn world, their life has no meaning, for their life's meaning is lived in the real world. Unlike a Pisces world which is lived in the places fairies live, or dreams happen.

So keep in mind, your Capricorn lives in that real world and no amount of jollying them along when things have gone pear-shaped will work. The basic, practical everyday items need to be sorted first, before anything fluffy is going to happen.

Saturn

To understand each Sun sign fully, we need to get an understanding of the images and ideas of their planetary ruler.

All the signs of the Zodiac have a planet that looks after them. We call this their planetary ruler.

The planet that 'looks after' Capricorn is Saturn. When we say ruler, we mean figuratively (not literally) the planet that has been deemed its boss. Don't get too bogged down with this word, just take it as the sign's 'Higher Self'.

Poor old Saturn. What a bad press that poor man has had! Death, destruction, delay and the Grim Reaper. Makes you want to shut the book and forget it all (if you've got planets in Gemini) but let us persevere and get to an understanding of Saturn and his attributes, because without it, we'll be lost and wandering.

Saturn's History

Saturn made its first appearance locally as a planet in the night sky as observed by the Babylonians. They thought about and looked at it thousands of years ago, and it is still making its way slowly across the sky. No change there. What has changed is our perception of it. In reality, as far as we know now, Saturn is the most distant planet visible to the naked eye and, unlike the earth, it has no surface to walk on and is made up of mostly gas and liquid. It is surrounded by beautiful rings made of the remains of small moons or asteroids that were torn apart millions of years ago.

The Babylonians called it the god Ninurta but not much was attributed to it in written texts as it was the faintest planet visible and slowest moving.

The sheer absence of variety in its appearance and location meant that, on purely functional grounds, it was far less useful than, say, the moon, as a source of omens. In this sense, Astrology was pragmatic. It worked with the material at hand, which might not reflect theological priorities.[13]

The Most Feared Planet

It wasn't until the Ancient Greeks adopted Astrology that Saturn was written about in any detail and by now he was now represented by the stern face of Kronos the father of Zeus. As Astrology progressed across the world, from East to West it took on different flavours and was written about in different ways until Astrology reached the West and Saturn became a definite negative part of the Birth Chart.

> In ancient and medieval times Saturn was the most feared of all planets. Its influence was thought to be almost entirely baneful, governing old age, sickness, death, imprisonment, and imparting dourness, coldness and inhibition.[2]

Saturn is the furthest planet from the Sun that can be seen with the naked eye, as we said before, which is why the ancients managed to plot its path and later write about it. In modern Astrology, Saturn is more seen as a restriction, not as the end-of-the-world-as-we-know-it. Mind you, when Saturn transits parts of your chart, you'll certainly feel its effects.

My private practice gets very busy when each Sun sign has Saturn going through their sign. The effects last for 2 years, so I get a sort of cycle of clients with various problems (depending on the sign they are). As I'm writing this, Saturn is transiting through the sign of Libra... so I'm seeing more Librans than usual.

When Saturn went through my sign, my first husband left me for another woman. That certainly felt destructive and negative.

Divorce is different from death, as in death you can grieve, while in divorce you're still grieving (if you don't get help) and the person who ended the relationship is still 'living' but dead to the other person. Well, that's how it felt for me.

To get further ideas about Saturn here are a few other Astrological authors' views.

Back to Felix Lyle in *The Instant Astrologer*. He titles it 'The Principle of Limitation' and goes on to say:

> In traditional Astrology Saturn was regarded as little short of evil… and associated with loss, hardship, delay, loneliness and death. A more grim repertoire is hard to imagine, but, given Saturn's mythology, it is hardly unwarranted, having castrated his father Uranus to seize control of the world… On the psychological level, Saturn's position in a chart reveals those fears and anxieties that through negative early conditioning make us feel deeply inadequate.

Mmm. Doesn't sound too friendly does he?

Let's check out Erin Sullivan's *Saturn in Transit, Boundaries of Mind, Body and Soul*, page 21:

> The renaissance of Saturn in occult philosophy stipulated that Saturn was to be rigorously attended to if one wished to come to terms with serious questions in life.

That word again: Serious!

Don't forget we can't separate the planet's images from us as human beings. We all exist in the same space. Astrology tries to define our place in the world on a personal and also spiritual level. The images of Saturn exist in us as humans. It wouldn't be natural for us to be happy all the time. To never feel fear, or get upset. The ancients wrote about the Saturn image in much more dramatic, drastic terms. Maybe they felt they had less control over their lives then, or less ability to cope with floods, famine and disease.

Do we do any better now?

Saturn is within all of us, it's just that some of us have more of it than others. We all have Saturn in our charts; in mine he's in the sign of Capricorn, so he's in his natural home, so I can empathise and comprehend those scary images, I just choose not to be overwhelmed by them.

And if you imagine, because that's all we can do, we can't prove it, just imagine that Saturn is the boss of Capricorn and therefore makes a Capricorn more of an earth being, we'll understand the sign better.

Chapter 2

How to Make a Chart

These days making a chart is simple. In the 'old days' you would have needed to have a really good knowledge of mathematics, the ability to calculate long complicated degrees and angles and access to the tables of planetary positions we call the Ephemeris.

You would then have to work out which sign was 'Rising' or 'Ascending' over the horizon and place it all into a circle, taking into account the fact that birth times and places throughout the world vary... not forgetting things like 'Summer Time' or 'War Time'. The advent of computers has reduced all of that calculation and hard work down to sometimes seconds rather than days.

Not that making something quicker makes it better, but you can get a computer program to do just about anything, provided the person who wrote the program knows what they're doing.

So, to find out more about the Capricorn in your life, we're going to use a Swiss website called www.astro.com.

Obviously, being Swiss makes it all the more accurate and it's also a website that Astrologers use, so you'll be in safe hands.

Equal House System

Make yourself an account, then go to the part of the site called 'Extended Chart Selection'. In this section of their website, halfway down the page is a section called 'Options' and underneath it says: 'House System' and if you look at it now it will say 'default'.

Click in this box and change it to 'equal'.

Don't just rush onto the site and gaily add data, as the default chart is called 'Placidus' and will come up with houses all of different sizes. This is too confusing for a beginner, and I think looks too strange to make sense.

For our example, we're going to use the data of J.R.R. Tolkien, the author of the wonderful *Lord of the Rings* books, born 3-1-1892, Bloemfontein, South Africa, 10pm.

Now, in the UK we use date/month/year but in the USA we use month/date/year so make doubly sure you're entering the right information. In our example above, J.R.R., who was actually called John Ronald Reuel, so we'll call him John to make things even easier, was born on the 3rd of January 1892.

Here is his birth chart.

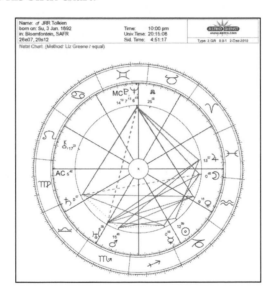

The lines in the center of the chart are either easy or challenging mathematical associations between each planet in the chart, so ignore them too. We only want 3 pieces of information.

The sign of the Ascendant, the sign the Moon is in and the house the Sun is in.

This is the abbreviation for the Ascendant: AC

This is the symbol for the Sun: ☉

This is the symbol for the Moon: ☽

The houses are numbered 1–12 in a anti-clockwise order.

These are the shapes representing the signs, so find the one that matches yours.

They are called glyphs.

Aries ♈

Taurus ♉

Gemini ♊

Cancer ♋

Leo ♌

Virgo ♍

Libra ♎

Scorpio ♏

Sagittarius ♐

Capricorn ♑

Aquarius ♒

Pisces ♓

The Elements

To understand your Capricorn fully, you must take into account which Element their Ascendant and Moon are in.

Each sign of the Zodiac has been given an element that it operates under: Earth, Air, Fire and Water. I like to think of them as operating at different 'speeds'.

The **Earth** signs are **Taurus**, **Virgo** and our friend **Capricorn**. The Earth Element is stable, grounded and concerned with practical matters and works best at a very slow, steady speed. (I refer to these in the text as 'Earthy'.)

The **Air** signs are **Gemini**, **Libra** and **Aquarius** (who is the 'Water-carrier' *not* a Water sign). The Air element enjoys ideas, concepts and thoughts. It operates at a faster speed than Earth, not as fast as Fire but faster than Water and Earth.

Imagine them as being medium speed.

The **Fire** signs are **Aries, Leo** and **Sagittarius**.
The Fire element likes action, excitement and can be very impatient. Their speed is *very* fast. (I refer to these as Firey i.e. Fire-Sign.)

The **Water** signs are **Cancer, Scorpio** and **Pisces**.
The Water element involves feelings, impressions, hunches and intuition. They operate faster than Earth but not as fast as Air. A sort of slow-medium speed.

Chapter 3

The Ascendant

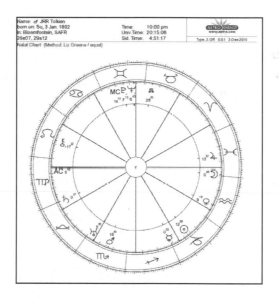

Here's John's chart again. This time I've removed all the aspect lines, just to make life even easier.

You will see he has his Ascendant in the sign of Virgo, making him good with detail, someone who likes to categorise and have things 'in place'.

The Ascendant or Rising Sign in Astrology is a term for the exact moment of birth and is calculated by the longitude and latitude of the location of birth and the time. If you were born in Brazil, you'd have a different Ascendant from someone born at the same time in Oslo. This is where you have to make sure that the time of birth you have is as accurate as possible.

Rodden Rating

A Gemini lady born in 1928 called Lois M. Rodden developed a method of recording birth times, so that professional Astrologers can be sure that the birth data they are using is correct. It is called 'The Rodden Rating'.14

If it has an 'A' rating, you can be sure that the birth time is reliable. A 'DD' rating, called 'Dirty Data', means there are two conflicting sources and further work is needed to find the accurate time.

If you are going to make the birth chart of the Capricorn in your life, you do need to have an accurate birth time as the Ascendant changes sign every two hours. This is because there are 24 hours in a day and 12 Sun signs, so the Ascending Sign will go through all the signs in a 24 hour period at a rate of one sign every two hours... and having a Gemini Ascendant is completely different from having a Cancer Ascendant which is the following sign.

Don't get confused, just get the right information and you'll be fine.

If you live in the UK, your Capricorn's birth time won't be recorded on their birth certificate, so don't bother looking. You'll have to get someone else in the family to help you as (generally) Mum would have been too busy giving birth to record the time. Dad can be quite good at remembering so ask him.

If you were born in Scotland you might be lucky as sometimes the birth time is recorded and if you were born in the USA, again the time is noted.

Sometimes people write the birth time down in a baby-book or family bible. I found a few members of my family in our bible, which was really helpful.

So, you now have your Capricorn's birth time. With our example John, the Virgo Ascendant made him good at detail, scrupulous about the finer points of writing as Virgo is ruled by the planet Mercury (which governs writing), and being 'fussy' or its more friendly term: 'accurate'.

So here are the various Ascendants with a Capricorn Sun sign. The different Ascendant will make your Capricorn operate in a different way. A Fire sign Ascendant is quicker, faster and speedier than an Earth sign Ascendant, so keep that in mind when you're reading your Capricorn's Ascendant.

It's funny, when you're trying to find quotes from people to demonstrate their Sun sign configurations, some indicators just can't be missed. There I was trying to find an example of something a Cancer Asc would say and I'd already got one in my Inbox from someone I know:

"I love cooking and I love cooking for friends coming to eat."

This is almost the exact phrase that Noel Tyl, an American Astrologer, used about cooking:

"Eating together affords a beautiful closeness at the end of any day. Doing it well creates memories."

As you can see, both quotes, the first from a journalist-mother-writer, the second from an Astrologer-cook both express the same sentiments... that they enjoy cooking because it brings their family (and friends that they feel close to) together... and the energies of Cancer is all about 'closeness'.

Aries Ascendant

"I've never had a humble opinion. If you've got an opinion, why be humble about it?"
Joan Baez, Sun in 10th

Aries is the first sign of the Zodiac and as such has a sort of 'me' attitude of looking after the 'self'. As a Fire sign and strong Ascendant for a Capricorn it will make the native fearless, determined and able to react swiftly to problems or situations. On the negative side it can lean towards self-centeredness, reactive behaviour, and a tendency to want to 'push the river'.

Taurus Ascendant

"The way I choose to show my feelings is through my songs."
Marianne Faithfull, Sun in 9th

Taurus is an Earth sign and all those words: slow, steady, dependable come to mind. Ruled by sensuous Venus they are more likely to enjoy the earthly pleasures of life, rather than the challenges. Your Capricorn will be much more practical and centred on things like money, a safe home and things they own. They will also indulge in all those forbidden delights like chocolate, sex and massage (not necessarily in that order).

Gemini Ascendant

"I wrote a thousand words every day."
Jack London, Sun in 8th

Here we have chatty Gemini, ruled by frisky Mercury the trickster. It's a more difficult combination for a Capricorn to absorb. On the one hand the Capricorn Sun wants responsibility and to climb high, while the Gemini Ascendant wants to talk and write and communicate. Put the two together and you get a 'serious communicator'.

Cancer Ascendant

"Eating together affords a beautiful closeness at the end of any day. Doing it well creates memories."
Noel Tyl, Sun in 7th

Squidgy Cancer, ruled by the Moon and a Water sign, makes a Capricorn more able to be sensitive to others. There will be domestic concerns, a need to feel their way around things, a desire for cosy settings and lasting relationships. Cooking scores highly too.

Leo Ascendant

"I am the greatest; I said that even before I knew I was."
Muhammad Ali, Sun in 6th

Leo is a Fire sign and certainly enjoys being the centre of attention. Combine that with Capricorn's aim for the top and nothing will stop this combination from seeking recognition for their brilliance. The desire to shine can be overwhelming and at odds with the Capricorn need to control their emotions.

Virgo Ascendant

"The door to the cabinet is to be opened using a minimum of 15 Kleenexes."
Howard Hughes, Sun in 4th

Another Earth sign, Virgo Ascendant creates a worry-filled demeanor. Needing to put things into boxes, wanting things ordered, explained, categorised. Feeling happier when their health is good, feeling bad when it isn't, then making it worse by worrying about it.

Libra Ascendant

"Staying focused is hard work and staying married is even harder."
Crystal Gayle, Sun in 3rd

Another Air sign, and ruled by smoochy Venus, this is the Asc that wants pastel colors, things looking beautiful, everything 'nice'. It's also the sign that rules relationships and the significant other will always be a concern.

Scorpio Ascendant

> *"The limit of trust can only be as deep as the limit of one's wounds."*
> Marcia Starck, Sun in 2nd

As the second Water sign in the Zodiac, anything to do with Scorpio has got a bad press. Words like secretive, intense and jealous are just a few. In fact a Scorpio Ascendant is jolly useful in this world we live in, as it stops the native from being too trusting and becoming taken-in. For a Capricorn it also means they won't give their heart or mind away… to anyone.

Sagittarius Ascendant

> *"The Lord can give, and the Lord can take away. I might be herding sheep next year."*
> Elvis Presley, Sun in 2nd

Here we have one of the most complicated combinations. The Fire sign Sagittarius is all about wide expansive ideas, ruled by benevolent Jupiter: trusting, philosophical and foot-in-the-mouth. For a Capricorn it makes them enjoy foreign lands, long-distance travel and a firm belief in 'something'. These two concepts of philosophy and responsibility can make the Capricorn need more 'fun' than they are comfortable with.

Capricorn Ascendant

> *"A revolution is not a dinner party, or writing an essay, or painting*

a picture, or doing embroidery."
Mao Tse-Tung, Sun in 12th

Now we reach the double-whammy. Capricorn Asc are happy in places and positions of great responsibility, content to accept life's hard knocks, willing to work for future goals. Capable of making 'big' decisions and difficult choices.

Aquarius Ascendant

"I'm pretty good with collaborative thinking. I work well with other people."
David Bowie, Sun 12th

As the final Air sign Asc, Aquarius makes the native dabble in all those weird and wonderful areas of life others might hardly ever touch. Nothing is too extreme, mental freedom is important and Friendships with a capital 'F'. Ruled by wacky Uranus, the Aquarius sign wants room to make play not war... and they'll want you there to help them. Their infectious enthusiasm for life will rub off on you.

Pisces Ascendant

"I can shed a tear at something as simple as a few words heard in a poem or on the radio, or a film or even when reading."
Client X, Sun 12th

The last sign of the Zodiac and ruled by fuzzy Neptune, Pisces Asc gives Capricorn's more harder side a squidgy exterior. Sensitivity is increased and the ability to soak-up all the sorrows of the world. Will feel bad if they witness something tragic. Will want to save dolphins and for everyone to take into account that sensitivity, which can become a problem if they are male.

Chapter 4

The Moon

If the Sun governs our conscious then the Moon governs our subconscious. It's like that in 'real life'. The Moon reflects the light from the Sun. So in Astrology we look at the Moon as being that emotional, feeling part of ourselves. Emotions are funny old things. I often wonder if animals have them. I sometimes think we'd get so much more accomplished if we didn't have any. If we could focus on our goals and not get dragged into wobbly, emotional messes, we'd live happier lives. But would we? Maybe it's all about the balance of things. Too much emotion and you get drained of all energy, not enough and you turn into Mr. Spock from Star Trek. I use a wonderful technique called EFT if I think my clients need some emotional release. Bit like letting some steam out of the emotional pressure-cooker of life. I tap a few rounds of EFT until the thing that's been bugging them bothers them less, then they go away more happy. I'm not a stoic believer by any means. Emotions are useful because they make the world more alive but equally too much emotion and things can get seriously out-of-hand. As the Moon changes sign every 2 days or so, it's important to determine your Capricorn's Moon sign accurately. Some days the Moon will change sign during that day, as the timing of the Moon has nothing to do with our clocks. So someone born in the morning of 1st January 1980 at 7am will have the Moon in the sign of Gemini and if they were born at 7pm it will now be in the sign of Cancer. And they are two totally different Moon signs. In our example John has his Moon in the sign of Pisces. Oh such a sensitive Moon for a man to have! What's also interesting is his soul-mate wife Edith had Sun in Aquarius, which isn't especially compatible with Capricorn, but she had Moon in Virgo (which linked nicely with John's Ascendant) and Venus and Mars in Pisces, which also linked nicely with John's own Moon sign in Pisces. We don't know what time Edith was born so we don't know her Ascendant but if you know it, do get in touch. Here are the Moon signs with a Capricorn Sun. Understanding someone's Moon sign helps us understand how they react to an emotional situation or even explains how they react emotionally.

The Dr. Edward Bach Flower Essences

In 1933 Dr. Edward Bach a medical doctor and Homeopath published a little booklet called *The Twelve Healers and Other Remedies*. His theory was that if the emotional component a person was suffering from was removed, their 'illness' would also disappear. I tend to agree with this kind of thinking as most illnesses (except being hit by a car) are preceded by an unhappy event or an emotional disruption that then sets into place the body getting out of sync. Removing the emotional issue and bringing a bit of stability into someone's life, when they are 'all over the place' certainly doesn't hurt and in some cases can improve the overall health so much that wellness resumes.

Knowing which Bach Flower Essence can help certain worries and anxieties gives your Capricorn more control over their lives (and yours if you are in the vicinity) and I've quoted Dr. Bach's actual words for each sign.

To use the Essences take 2 drops from the stock bottle and put them into a glass of water and sip. I tend to recommend putting them into a small water bottle, and sipping them throughout the day, at least 4 times. For young children, do the same.

Remember to seek medical attention if symptoms don't get better and/or seek professional counseling.

Aries Moon

"Like electricity, the Light is everywhere, but one must know how to activate it. I have come for that."
Mother Meera

Aries is a Fire sign and likes to be first in everything it does, so a Capricorn having this sort of Moon will be in a permanent dilemma. On the one hand they are positive, upbeat, focused and competitive; on the other they want to work towards that elusive future goal and are happy to be in the background. What happens in reality is they spend some time being one thing and confused about the other parts. Balance is captured when they learn to acknowledge their needs but also the needs of others.

Bach Flower Essence Impatiens:

'Those who are quick in thought and action and who wish all things to be done without hesitation or delay.'

Taurus Moon

"I hate pornography… I haven't even got a pornograph!"
Kenny Everett

As an Earth sign Taurus needs their physical world organised before anything else will fall into place and coupled with the Earth sign Sun Capricorn increases the need for a practical, earth-based world. Ruled by Venus, the Goddess of Love, they love sexy, tactile handling. Chocolates go down well, so do soft velvety clothes and sensual indulgence.

Bach Flower Essence Gentian:

'Those who are easily discouraged. They may be progressing well in the affairs of their daily life, but any small delay or hindrance to

progress causes doubt and soon disheartens them.'

Gemini Moon

"Paul has no friends and it's driving me mad."
Heather Mills

The Air sign Gemini is ruled by tricky Mercury the God of communication, so being able to chat, circulate, gossip, converse are all important issues. Your Capricorn with this Moon will love stories, short journeys and the ability to talk about how they feel. If you want a Gemini Moon to spill the beans, take them for a short drive and they will happily tell you things they would feel embarrassed or awkward about face-to-face. Maybe it's the fact that the two of you will be facing the same way, as opposed to each other, that allows this Moon sign to express comfortably how they feel.

This Essence comes under the heading 'For Those Who Suffer Uncertainty' (which Libra and Gemini both suffer from).

Bach Flower Essence Cerato:

'Those who have not sufficient confidence in themselves to make their own decisions.'

Cancer Moon

"Gravitation is not responsible for people falling in love."
Isaac Newton

Cancer is a Water sign and on the Zodiac circle is the sign opposite to Capricorn, so here we have someone with a squishy, tender inside. Like a Turkish delight, soft and sweet to the core. They will be concerned with the family, their offspring, the food cupboard and Ruled by the Moon, nurturing and caring.

Bach Flower Essence Clematis:

'Living in the hopes of happier times, when their ideals may come true.'

Leo Moon

"I present myself in a strong, careful, and confident fashion."
Noel Tyl

The fiery Leo Moon makes the stern Capricorn more interested in their image and like all leonine images a 'leader', 'confident' and ruled by the Sun, wanting to 'shine'. It can be a hard act to pull off: being strong, careful and confident without being brash, brassy and vulgar. There are a number of famous people with this signature, not all are tasteful. If your Capricorn has this Moon, do make sure they feel acknowledged and respected and a little flattery will be appreciated.

Bach Flower Essence Vervain:

'Those with fixed principles and ideas, which they are confident are right.'

Virgo Moon

"That's the funniest thing about portraying certain things on screen, sitting next to your parents and they get to see this glimpse of me kissing another guy."
Kate Bosworth

Another Earth sign, Virgo is ruled by inquisitive Mercury. With your Capricorn's Moon placed here, they are going to want to know 'Why?' As Virgo also likes to have specifics organised and catalogued, they will worry and fret less if they can have things 'sorted'. Don't leave things to chance, plan as much as possible and keep health issues under control… and stop smoking.

My most often prescribed remedy, as Virgo Moon, Sun or Asc are my best customers. It comes under the heading 'Over-Sensitive to Influences and Ideas'.

Bach Flower Essence Centuary:

'Their good nature leads them to do more than their own share of work and they may neglect their own mission in life.'

Libra Moon

"I'm sad about this, but we shouldn't have been married in the first place."
Nicolas Cage

As a Venus ruled sign, Libra is about fairness, beauty and close, personal relationships. When they're not in one, they're unhappy bunnies. For a Capricorn who does stiff upper lip very well, admitting that they want to be close to someone might prove a tad difficult. It'll happen; it just might take some time.

Bach Flower Essence Scleranthus:

'Those who suffer from being unable to decide between two things, first one seeming right then the other.'

Scorpio Moon

"I've test-run all the underwear, too. It's all very sexy, but not nasty-sexy, glamorous-sexy. Not vulgar."
Kate Moss

As Scorpio is such a secretive sign, try not to pry and also resist the temptation to ask too many questions. It's a happy place for

Capricorn to have their Moon as the two signs Cap and Scorp get on well. To an outsider they will seem deep, dark and mysterious, which they are and they also have X-ray BS sensors. You can't lie to this combination, so don't even try and once you've gained their trust, don't break it as you'll never, ever be forgiven.

Bach Flower Essence Chicory:

'They are continually correcting what they consider wrong and enjoy doing so.'

Sagittarius Moon

"I stand up for what I believe. I don't know if it's always paid off for me, because I've been ridiculed and humiliated."
Kevin Costner

If you want to know the truth, ask someone with a Sagittarius Moon. They will also tell you that you're fat, that you've got food on your face and your feet smell. They won't be judging you but they'll give it to you straight. This is a more tricky combination for a Capricorn, who are mostly the epitome of diplomacy. Sag is ruled by upbeat benevolent Jupiter who was the God of Gods and tells it as it is. Oh, and they'll also use the word 'believe' a lot.

This Essence comes under the heading 'Over-Sensitive to Influences and Ideas'. Reading something upsetting will influence them a great deal.

Bach Flower Essence Agrimony:

'They hide their cares behind their humor and jesting and try to bear their trials with cheerfulness.'

Capricorn Moon

"It's the poignancy and sadness in things that gets to me."
Tracey Ullman

Here we have the Earth sign Capricorn Sun, joined to the Moon, so this increases all the key words for a Capricorn = Stoic, Responsible and Serious. However they will also have a crackingly good sense of humor. Maybe dry, but witty. If they don't fall into the black-hole of depression their dual nature will ensure a pragmatic and amusing look at life.

Bach Flower Essence Mimulus:

'Fear of worldly things, illness, pain, accident, poverty, of dark, of being alone, of misfortune. They secretly bear their dread and do not speak freely of it to others.'

Aquarius Moon

"I worry about the issues, so the focus should be on moving this ball forward, on the greater good of our kids, the environment, and who cares what they say about me."
Michelle Obama

The Air sign Aquarius Moon is concerned with the wider, altruistic world. They want us to join hands in harmony and work towards the nirvana of co-operation. Ruled by wacky Uranus the planet of individuality means they will also value freedom with a capital 'F' so don't try and tie them down. Ideas are important and the Capricorn Sun will ensure those ideas are put to good use rather than bounced around to all and sundry.

Bach Flower Essence Water Violet:

'For those who like to be alone, very independent, capable and self-

reliant. They are aloof and go their own way.'

Pisces Moon

"I took drugs because we all took drugs."
Marianne Faithfull

As the last sign of the Zodiac and as one of the most sensitive Water signs, the Pisces Moon ruled by Neptune can bring allusion and delusion. On the one hand they want to be connected to all that is good with the world and on the other might indulge in all that the world produces that is bad. One thing is for sure, they love the mystical and psychic. And on a good day will intuit your feelings and ring you when you're down, and on a bad day will fall with you into the abyss.

Bach Flower Essence Rock Rose:

'For cases where there even appears no hope or when the person is very frightened or terrified.'

Chapter 5

The Houses

Now, if the Moon represents our inner self, and the Sun represents our ego or outer self, then the location of that Sun and the other planets in the chart is an interesting concept. The houses in Astrology represent different areas of life. They're called houses because they become the 'home' of each of the 10 planets we use. They used to be called 'mansions' which sounds a bit posh and isn't used much anymore. Where your Capricorn's Sun is located in their personal Birth Chart is quite important and without an accurate birth time is impossible. So if you don't know the birth time, please ignore this chapter.

When the first Astrologers decided to identify and convert the location on the planets into a personal expression, the Birth Chart was born. If the Ascendant represents the time and location of birth, our first breath, the moment we hit the planet and then the Sun is going to be somewhere on our little earth/planet map. But where? In John's example, because his Ascendant is Virgo, his Sun will have to be either in the 4th or 5th house, if we're using the Equal House system.

In John's case his Sun is in the 5th house the house of creativity and romance. And he certainly was a creative individual. He wrote and was the author of over 35 publications. The word prolific comes to mind. The Lord of the Rings has over 470,000 words alone. And this was before computers. Now, the houses are a funny old thing and one that confuses so many people that try to understand Astrology and instantly puts them off. What's a house? What does it mean? Why do they go round the wheel anti-clockwise? If you imagine the centre of the chart is the Earth, where we live, the Ascendant is the part of the Universe that's in line with the eastern horizon, where the Sun comes up every day. However, if you were born later in the day, or earlier in the day, the Sun wouldn't be on your Ascendant; it will be further around the circle.

The First House, House of Personality

*"One common mistake is to think that one reality is **the** reality. You must always be prepared to leave one reality for a greater one."*
Mother Meera

Having the Capricorn Sun in the first house ensures personal confidence as it relates to the 'self', is sort of an 'I am the centre of the world feeling'. They are open, fearless, more capable of withstanding opposition and generally very self-assured. 'Take me as you find me' should be their motto.

(Ascendant Capricorn or Sagittarius)

The Second House, House of Money, Material Possessions and Self-Worth

"We never had any money or nothin', but we never were hungry, you know. That's something to be thankful for."
Elvis Presley

This is the house that represents the things that we own. The practical world. Energy will be spent on accumulating possessions or financial security. Enjoyment will be found from holding, touching, truly experiencing things... tactile experiences like massage are generally treasured.

(Ascendant Sagittarius or Scorpio)

The Third House, House of Communication & Short

Journeys

"Words have no power to impress the mind without the exquisite horror of their reality."
Edgar Allan Poe

Like the third sign Gemini, the third house wants to engage with others by communicating with them. They would need a mobile phone, access to letters, telephones, conversations and all forms of communication. Being able to chat or write satisfies this house. As it also governs short journeys having some means of transport is good.

(Ascendant Scorpio or Libra)

The Fourth House, House of Home, Family & Roots

"Now I understand what divorce is really about, particularly when children are involved."
Annie Lennox

This is where the home becomes important. 'Family' in all its varied combinations will be a high priority. Cooking, snuggling up to others, pets, being close to significant others and the domestic world are all important.

(Ascendant Libra or Virgo)

The Fifth House, House of Creativity & Romance

"Vicars, MPs and lawyers were amongst those who considered me to be the best hostess in London."
Cynthia Payne

The fifth house is concerned with being able to shine. Being the center of attention is also a plus. Red carpets, heaps of praise and

appreciative recognition keeps this combination happy.
(Ascendant Virgo or Leo)

The Sixth House, House of Work & Health

"I do have a sense that the message of flowers in flower essences could 'save the world'… save our health."
Client Z

The sixth house has its focus on everything related to health. It also is the work that we do. The Capricorn Sun here will want to be well, healthy and organised. It's not unheard of for them to work in the health and healing sector.
(Ascendant Leo or Cancer)

The Seventh House, House of Relationships & Marriage

"I am not alone while my love is near me."
Sandy Denny

The Capricorn Sun here will want to share their life with another significant other. Being single won't wash. Until their close personal relationship is organised life feels bleak. When attached to someone life has new meaning.
(Ascendant Cancer or Gemini)

The Eighth House, House of Life Force in Birth, Sex, Death & After-Life

"I would rather be ashes than dust! I would rather be a superb meteor, every atom of me in magnificent glow, than a sleepy and permanent planet."
Jack London
The intensity of the eighth house with the Capricorn Sun makes

an individual who is strong in character and un-swayed from their life's mission. Boredom is not on the menu! The ability to focus exclusively on one thing at a time can bring great results.

(Ascendant Gemini or Taurus)

The Ninth House, House of Philosophy & Long Distance Travel

"The voice of God, if you must know, is Aretha Franklin's."
Marianne Faithfull

Provided that the ninth house Sun in Capricorn can philosophise about life's true meaning all is well. Foreign countries, long journeys, and an interest in other cultures will be expressed here. Keep passports at the ready.

(Ascendant Taurus or Aries)

The Tenth House, House of Social Identity & Career

"You don't get to choose how you are going to die or when. You can only decide how you're going to live."
Joan Baez

This is Capricorn's natural home so you would expect the individual to be focused on their career and how they feel others perceive them. Being able to be recognised in their chosen field no matter how long this may take will guide them to success.

(Ascendant Aries or Pisces)

The Eleventh House, House of Social Life & Friendships

"In school you learn about American history through battles, but I learned about the United States and the people of the United States through this music and the songs I sing."

Odetta Holmes

With the Capricorn Sun in the 11th house individuals will want, no *need*: friends groups, organisations, affiliations, societies that they can/will be members of. They don't see themselves in isolation to the world, they are part of it. Friendships are top of the list, so is charitable work and uniting the planet.

(Ascendant Pisces or Aquarius)

The Twelfth House, House of Spirituality

"People expect Janis Joplin to be a tough bitch, and say I start talking to them like a lonely little girl – that's not in their image of me – they don't see it."
Janis Joplin

I have noticed a lot of my clients who have Sun in the 12th really don't like living in the 'real world'. It all seems too painful and insensitive. The 12th house, like the star sign Pisces, wants to merge with the fairies and angels and escape to Never Never Land. They feel better where they have somewhere to escape to emotionally, be that the beach, on a hilltop, or in a nice warm bath.

(Ascendant Aquarius or Capricorn)

Chapter 6

The Problems

To fully help your Capricorn it's good to understand the definition of what help they might need. The sort of things that might be a problem now or become a problem later. The everyday things that I hear in private practice are varied but here are a few examples:

My Capricorn doesn't seem happy and is so gloomy it's driving me mad what should I DO?

This must be my most asked question by partners of Capricorns. While I can offer some practical advice for the suffering Capricorn (see Chapters 7 & 8) I tend to focus on the person who is *receiving* the negative onslaught.

First of all learn what sign-type you are and do all you can to make *yourself* happy.

If you are an Air sign (Aquarius, Gemini or Libra) you are easily distracted, so do something or go somewhere that will take your mind off what is happening. You'll feel better in some pleasant company, so get some friends round, or go and meet and enjoy the company of people who will lift your spirits. Don't focus on, or talk about your grumpy Capricorn, as it will only make you feel worse and more disempowered. Change the subject.

If you are a fellow Earth sign (Taurus or Virgo), concentrate on completely ignoring what is happening. You can't make it any better and you're likely to make everything worse, so just get on doing the things you like. Involve yourself with physical task-based activities: dig the garden, do some cooking, eat nice food, get someone to give you a massage or surround yourself with other members of the family/friends that can enjoy these activities with you.

If you are a Water sign (Cancer, Scorpio or Pisces), you possess the ability to actually help the unhappy Capricorn as your empathy levels are heightened. You can do all those lovely fluffy things that a grumpy Capricorn will secretly enjoy such as: massage, alternative healing, cooking and empathy. However, as a Water sign you also run the risk of *becoming* part of the problem so a little emotional detachment would be good.

If you are a Fire sign (Aries, Leo or Sagittarius) your levels of patience will be rather low and no amount of jollying will bring results. You could offer some form of assistance by inviting your gloomy Capricorn to join you in some sort of competitive sport. However, they might be too gloomy to even contemplate this kind of action, so go and do something physical yourself and thrash your feelings out on the tennis court, the football/soccer pitch, rugby ground or similar.

My Capricorn is so focused on his/her career I feel left out.
A Capricorn's career is very important once they have resolved all practical issues including money, home-building, and children making. They also have the ability to separate work and home life. Again consider what element you are: Earth, Air, Fire or Water and what your needs are. Michelle Obama is a Capricorn and supported her husband Barak in becoming president of the USA. Their early careers were very conjoined as they both worked in law. I can't see her complaining too much about his work/life balance, as the benefits for her are considerable. If your Capricorn is very ambitious and you are not, there is no good complaining. It might just be best to part. You do have choices.

My Capricorn is so focused on his/her family I feel left out.
This is slightly different from the previous problem but is one I often hear in private practice. Are you really left out? Or are you

choosing to be left out? And do you have difficulties with sharing? Do you consider yourself possessive? A Capricorn's family is their raison d'être, something they would have made clear right at the beginning. I'm sure with a little practise you can involve yourself with their family too.

My Capricorn isn't exciting enough for me.

I tend to hear this when I'm dealing with a Fire sign, or clients with Fire sign planets. What you classify as exciting a Capricorn might find exhausting. Lengthy and dramatic emotional displays are not Capricorn territory. Measured and sensible responses are. They are not devoid of feelings but they won't waste precious energy on seemingly unnecessary emotion. Remember the Stoics in Chapter 1? Being overly emotional can prevent success. There is a time and place for everything. Are you aware that your Capricorn can be exciting? I know a Capricorn who does white-water rafting, mountain trekking and physical activities that can leave you breathless. He isn't, however, on the phone to his friends at the bus stop crying about something someone said. Please don't accuse, ever, a Capricorn of being boring; spend your energy instead on seeing and experiencing their exciting but modest side.

My Capricorn only seems to like people older than him/herself.

This is rather a truism. Capricorns respect the knowledge and wisdom that old age can bring. Isn't that rather a nice trait to have? To treat our elders as wise beings? Why does old age have to equal senility? If you are a Gemini – the Peter Pan of the Zodiac, the child who will never grow up – you might find this difficult. Don't let it ruin your opinion of them. Old age can and does bring wisdom and you might find as your Capricorn gets older, they become more childlike and are more likely to enjoy younger company.

My Capricorn doesn't talk to me... enough.

This was a problem for a Sagittarius client of mine:

I definitely need help in getting my Capricorn boyfriend to be a little more communicative. He's lots of fun when I'm with him, but he can go for days and days without actually texting or calling me. I'm trying to take it slow (as you suggested); but after 6 months of dating, I was hoping he might open up and get a bit better at the communication side of things. Do you have any tips of how to handle this? I've mentioned the subject to him briefly in a light-hearted kind of way, and he admitted that previous girlfriends and even family members have said the same thing about him, but he then said that he doesn't really think he is ever going to change. Do you think he is just being honest or does this just mean that he doesn't want to make the effort?

As it turned out they parted company because Ms. Sagittarius didn't appreciate the true Capricorn spirit. No fault on either part. Sometimes we have to have a negative experience to appreciate what we truly want and in this example Ms. Sagittarius would have been better off with an Air sign, maybe even a Gemini as they can be quite chatty.

The reason Mister Capricorn wasn't phoning every day was because in his mind there was nothing to say. Capricorn isn't going to give you a running commentary of what they're up to. And he was being completely honest when he said he was never going to change. The thought of leopards changing spots comes to mind. Ms. Sagittarius now knows that what she's looking for in a partner is someone who will talk to her every day, or even three or four times a day. Even people who have no belief or understanding in Astrology will find difficulties in relationships when they're dating or marrying someone who doesn't have the same, or compatible Astrological life-philosophy.

Chapter 7

The Solutions

Now that you've learned a little about what a Capricorn is, we're now going to cover the most important part of this book, How to Cheer Up a Capricorn.

Simple.

Don't!

"What?!" I hear you cry. "They've been in a terrible slump for 6 months, they've been listening to the same piece of music for weeks, they've grunted every time I've spoken to them. How can you get this far and tell me they don't *need* cheering-up, what do you MEAN??"

It's simple; Capricorns are serious people.

And serious people take things seriously. And taking things seriously means there is no facade, a sort of 'take me as you find me' type of attitude. And to be serious is to be genuine. Not pretend, not fake, not plastic, not imaginary but real.

If we compare this to Pisces, who lives with the fairies, creating a non-existent world that is fluffy and gentle but can't pay the bills or remember where tea towel is; or we compare this to Aquarius who lives in their mind, creating ideas to unify the world and for everyone to be friendly, we'll see that *someone* has to live in the real world, has to pay the bills, has to knit the woolly vests and knickers for the poor families, has to stay focused on practical, real solutions. It's just that, this level of reality can be difficult for other signs to understand. So what I'm saying here is: find the place where you're happy, and you're having fun and maybe, just maybe your Capricorn will see you enjoying yourself and want to join you!

When Will I Ever Be Happy?

"I HATE being a Capricorn Woman: life is full of Stupid lessons. I heard that being born under this cursed sign means we gotta learn some lessons. Well I never wanted to.

I hate my luck and blame my parents for bringing me in this world under the Capricorn sun.

Unfortunately it is not only me, all the Capricorns (especially women: Elin Woods, Sienna Miller, and so many others) are not happy. People say that Capricorns are prone to depression, but why are we? It is because of our damn sign, which gives us a s*** load of depressive things in life.

I don't know when I will ever be happy. I know happiness is what you make out of your life, but what do you do when there are lessons to learn every step of the way? You get tired of it.

Friends? I do not have ANY at ALL. lol yea it might sound exaggerating, but trust me on that LOL.

The ones who I thought were my "FRIENDS" all betrayed me one way or the other. For example, I was madly in love with a Scorpio, for years; when he finally asked me out, I was so out of my mind and scared, that I blew it, but things weren't that bad, since we were friends. But what happened? My supposedly "best" friend talked him into breaking up with me and he thought that since she is my best friend, it was the right thing for me.

But not only that, now I am married to another Capricorn. He is jobless, loses his jobs wherever he works, in a few months; and the saddest part is I feel secure when he doesn't work, since he always says he will leave, because he is not happy with me.

I am at school, with a scholarship. Had a chance to go to an Ivy League, but another Capricorn man talked me out of going there. Now I am at XXX, thinking that I would save money, which is actually not the case.

As for my family, I really feel bad about my parents, they are old now, and still supporting us including my ungrateful (sometimes) husband.

And guess what? They are BOTH Capricorns as well. My Mom 30th December, me 31st December, my Dad 1st January. Is that fated or what? Almost scary.

We are from a very conservative community, so when I married an Italian guy everyone was shocked, so having a divorce will be worse for my family. So I am taking whatever my husband is throwing at me and my family, (but that is not frequent).

And another thing is respect. I don't think we have seen much, which really bothers me; we feel like we are an isolated family."

Here we have a completely unsatisfied Capricorn woman. She wants to have a family, a friend or two, a nice marriage and happy parents. She has none of those things and this has gone deeply into her sense of self-worth.

In the example above, our Capricorn lady wants respect but she knows she can't have it until her marriage is firmer and her husband has a job. But then she worries that if he *does* have a job, he'll leave her because *he* isn't happy, so this is a horrible dilemma. She's trying to improve herself by studying but as she's not where she wants to be, which is the 'Ivy League', she's even more despondent.

Ivy League schools are often viewed by the public as some of the most prestigious universities worldwide and are often ranked amongst the best universities in the United States and worldwide. (Taken from the Wikipedia page on Ivy Schools)

So, now she's studying at somewhere cheaper but it's not bringing what she wanted, which is respect. So two things are deeply bothering her, that fact that she is unhappy and also that she is not respected and she can't gain respect until her life is a little more organised and stable.

For a Capricorn to 'be happy' and to cheer them up, they

NEED to have a stable family unit. It doesn't matter how that unit manifests. It can be Mom and Dad in a shack with rice for dinner but because of the 'support' of the 'family unit' everything will be OK.

Take a Capricorn away from that family unit, remove their parents, their children, their husbands or wives and you're on really shaky ground.

This is completely different from our friends the Aquarians, who won't bother at all about 'the family' because for them, the family is universal and never-ending. For a Capricorn the family is their life.

The Capricorns I see in my private practice come to see me if there is a threat of divorce, if their parents die 'before their time', if their children aren't fitting into their perceived vision of 'correct living' or if they lose their jobs or position in life. I will advise them and we'll talk about how to correct the missing elements.

Now, it would be a completely different matter if your Capricorn said they were feeling down, or asked you to help them cheer up, or strongly indicated that they needed help... and if they have please see below on how to help.

But, and this is a BIG BUT, not every Capricorn will need cheering.

Let me explain.

Humor is different to different people. What you find extremely funny, your friend/lover/parent/sibling might find completely un-funny. It's the same with general disposition. Maybe it's YOU that needs cheering-up? Maybe YOU need something light and fluffy in your life?

Especially if you're an Air sign.

I'll give you an example. My mother is an Aquarius (I wrote about her a bit in *How to Bond with an Aquarius*). My youngest sister is a Capricorn and they have lived together for more than 40 years. She also has Down's syndrome (but that's got nothing to do with what I'm about to tell you).

Mum occasionally complains that my sister doesn't seem happy, and I have to explain she's perfectly happy. She won't be running around the house, gaily dancing or singing the latest songs on the radio. She won't be humming a little tune (like my mum does), she won't be on the phone chatting to all-and-sundry and she certainly won't be thinking about 'interesting things to do', that's Aquarian territory. No, my little sister will be writing letters to her family (an important aspect of her life) and TV stars, watching Dr. Who on the telly, reading her magazine subscription to the RSPB (she likes birds), looking forward to the next family event or even eating, sleeping, washing and getting dressed.

Sensible, practical occupations.

For an Aquarius having to even *think* about eating, sleeping, washing and getting dressed would be enough to tip them over the edge. In fact anything related to the physical world in all its mess, dirt, feelings, soap/water, digestion... No, no, no!!

So, if you're an Aquarius, this is for you to read and understand: your Capricorn is NOT unhappy. They don't need you to cheer them up with happy fluffiness and frivolity.

They might be sad, or anxious, or slow or quiet or thoughtful, or thinking-about-how-to-get-the-balloon-that-Piglet-gave Eeyore-in-and-out of the 'Useful Pot' that Pooh gave him on his birthday.

Life is *slower* when you're a Capricorn, much slower than being a Fire sign. That's not to say that a Capricorn can't be speeded up by having some Fire in their chart. I've included plenty of examples of people with Fire sign planets in their charts in this book but overall Capricorn wants to take their time and savour the moment.

So what do you do if your Capricorn has admitted that they are unhappy and has *asked* you to help them feel less down? Has *asked* to be 'Cheered Up'?

Well, first of all you need to do the appropriate type of cheering depending of their individual chart characteristics. So here is a sensible, do-able list of suggestions to help your Capricorn.

I've divided them into the different Ascendants and Moons.

Aries Asc or Moon

Take your Capricorn for walk, the longer the better. Walking boots, weatherproofs, sensible shoes, some food for the journey (if you're a Taurus), some money and nothing else. You don't need a mobile phone, iPod, map or compass. Just an expanse of outdoors and fresh open air. If your Cappie is very physically orientated you can do something energetic and/or sporty. They won't want to talk so don't even try, just focus on the physical experience.

Taurus Asc or Moon

The best way to help a double Earth sign is in a practical, sensible, down to earth way. As Taurus enjoys food and sensuous luxury, indulging in some chocolate-cake-therapy is a good option. They will also want their finances organised, so get out the calculator and work out the maths. If you're any good at massage, this will be a great help. If you're not, book your Capricorn in for a session with a good local therapist. Again, keep conversation to the minimum.

Gemini Asc or Moon

This is the sign combination that does need to chat. They would also like a little trip, so jump in the car and drive somewhere and on the journey your Gemini Moon/Asc Cappie will spill the beans. Don't try and offer too many solutions as this will add to the turmoil; instead recommend some good reading material that your wobbly Cappie can enjoy and listen, listen, listen, as your Cappie will want to talk about how they are feeling.

Cancer Asc or Moon

Oodles of sympathy are needed here. Cancer is a Water sign, and makes a person who really needs EMPATHY. You can't just cluck and look interested here. Unless you have suffered what Cancer has, you're out of the game. Best strategy is to get the kettle on, take a deep breath, turn off your mobile, look calm and sympathetic, lean into the Cancer/Cappie space, mirror body language, and get the tissues handy. Cancer/Cappies need to cry and will generally feel much better afterwards.

Leo Asc or Moon

The Second Fire sign of the Zodiac, Leo/Cappie needs an audience, and will want to dramatically act out how they are feeling. Ignore this at your peril. Their only reason for exaggeration is because they fear rejection, so lay down the metaphorical red carpet and allow them to be King/Queen for the day. They are unlikely to tell you exactly how sad they feel but deep inside the drama is a sad and lonely little child.

Virgo Asc or Moon

Now, I was tempted to say get the doctor round as Virgo/Cappie is so concerned with their health. When upset though, a Virgo/Cappie will fret and fret and fret, so you feel like screaming "CALM DOWN"... which obviously is not a sensible solution. Small steps to recovery are better such as cutting down sugar intake, ceasing to smoke, eating healthy food and avoiding negativity. Meditation works wonders.

Libra Asc or Moon

Here you might need the tissues again. You will also need calm and tranquil, pleasant surroundings. Libra/Cappie is very sensitive to their environment and as Libra is 'ruled' by Venus they respond better to beauty. They might need gentle questioning, having tea is good but far better would be a big bunch of roses or a gentle aromatherapy massage. Things need to be balanced for Libra/Cappie and fair. Everyone has to take a share of what is going on. Point out that if they consider everyone else's point of view, they will only tire themselves even more, so it would be best to find just one strategy to 'move forward' with.

Scorpio Asc or Moon

This is the sign combination where you will need strength and focus. It's no good being fluffy here. Intense and dramatic solutions work best and I tend to recommend things like writing letters and burning them or other harmless activities rather than getting into fights, or legal spats.

> *I have absolutely no pleasure in the stimulants in which I sometimes so madly indulge. It has not been in the pursuit of pleasure that I have periled life and reputation and reason. It has been the desperate attempt to escape from torturing memories, from a sense of insupportable loneliness, and a dread of some strange impending doom.*
> Edgar Allan Poe as quoted in Meyers, '89

Your Scorpio/Cappie will probably go on a wild alcohol fuelled drinking spree, or risk their life with drugs, but provided that you offer a safe space of solace, they will eventually return to a place of normality. Allow about two weeks.

Sagittarius Asc or Moon

Do not give advice to a Sag/Cappie, you will only make them worse. They have all the answers, they're just hidden somewhere under a pile of paperwork. They know exactly what's wrong with them, they're not unhappy, they just struggling with indigestion/heartburn/migraine. The best solution it is to book a nice foreign trip. The more distant the better. Failing that get them to bring out old photographs of previous holidays and spend some time together looking at them.

Capricorn Asc or Moon

Again I do not recommend advice giving. This will only lead to conflict. Instead spend some time focusing on distant ancestors. Talking about, remembering, reminiscing about grandfathers, great-grandfathers and long ago relatives will help put things into perspective. If you're any good at family history now's your chance to shine. Discussing how things used to be and living the future through the past is your best tactic. Visiting museums, learning about ancient cultures and respecting old/folk traditions will help your double Capricorn immensely.

Aquarius Asc or Moon

This is where thinking and ideas come into play. The wackier the better. Something that combines friendship and seniority. Suggestions would be joining a humanist group, or campaigning for human rights. Get your Aqua/Cappie to shoot off a few letters of complaint to various well-respected publications. Or write a poem, or sing a song, something creative, artistic, or just plain daft; something, anything that will get them thinking about 'unity', their favourite subject.

Pisces Asc or Moon

> *I mean there has to be a purpose... there's got to be a reason... why I was chosen to be Elvis Presley... I swear to God, no one knows how lonely I get. And how empty I really feel.*[9]

This is the sign combination of sensitivity. Please be gentle with them. Imagine they are beings with gossamer wings, angels in disguise, beings from another planet, and you'll have more of an idea of how to help them. They won't really listen to what you tell them, they'll sense it, but you might feel that nothing sank in. It did. It will just take a while to filter through all the other 'stuff' that is in their heads. Light a candle, burn incense, lay out some

Angel Cards or use some other form of divination to help you. If they're not into the esoteric, good old-fashioned religion works well... and prayer.

Chapter 8

Cheering-Up Tactics

As this is a helpful little book, I'll now go through the various types of Capricorns you'll come across in real life, everything from your child to your parents. We'll discuss and get to understand all the different scenarios that knowing a Capricorn can bring and the different sorts of people you might come across in real life.

Your Capricorn Child

If you are the parent to a Capricorn child, your family life will not be complicated by rebellion or disobedience. It does of course depend on your sign and that of your partner. As long as you provide a safe and secure environment, with sensible rules and lots of family interaction, you won't go too far wrong.

A Capricorn child will definitely appreciate being treated as a grown-up from an early age. Giving minor responsibilities such as emptying the rubbish (trash), feeding the family pet/s or washing-up in return for pocket money will enable your child to learn that Saturn-ruled activities bring benefits, in this case financial.

Be aware that these responsibilities must not extend to your Capricorn child becoming a parent and you becoming the child. It's quite easy for roles to be reversed and I have seen it happen. This results in the Capricorn child never really enjoying their babyhood and growing quite anxious.

Generally speaking, your Capricorn child will enjoy the input of grandparents. Here we have Suzie who had a horrible time with her parents and was rescued emotionally by her grandparents:

"My grandparents treated me differently than most adults did. I felt like I didn't have to censor myself around them. They understood that I grew up very fast, and they treated me like an adult, whereas other people in my family (especially my father and his family) treated me like a child. I think that all-in-all, my grandparents and I share similar world views, and I just feel at home with them! They have always given me uncensored advice, but accept me for who I am and let me be me."

Your Capricorn child will also enjoy the concept that they are contributors to the efficient running of the home, and are valued members of the family. To say to a Capricorn child that they are not 'old enough' to do/be something insults their intelligence and ability. Better to allow them a small amount of gentle responsibility at an early age, than have it forced upon them when they grow up and leave home.

Your Capricorn Boss

Assuming of course that you know your boss' birth date, you can make your working life much easier by applying the standard Capricorn principles: be sensible, be responsible and produce results.

If you are even a teeny bit flighty, you'll find your Capricorn boss will overlook you for promotion. If you want to succeed with him/her as your superior, find out the things that they admire and replicate them.

You will also win Brownie points if you remember your boss' wife/husband's birthday/wedding anniversary.

Remember also that your Capricorn boss will not be breathing down your neck. They're not concerned with keeping tabs on your every movement, but they will expect any results that you have promised. Your word is your bond. Try and keep any work discussions to that which is practical and down-to-earth. Avoid the temptation (if you're an Air sign) to get into arguments or disagreements about ideas. This is not the Capricorn way of doing things. You will be expected to work hard and equally you will be rewarded for doing so.

Your (male) Capricorn Lover

To have a successful relationship with your Capricorn lover depends entirely on your own Sun sign, and/or Moon sign.

There are certain sign combinations that work really well, Capricorn/Scorpio being one of them. Both signs are endowed with a significant amount of self-control, something that both signs respect.

Things get difficult when Capricorn is paired with an Air sign:

"The worst part is that I seem to be attracted to them. I've dated several Aquarian women and it's never ended well. I'm the typical Capricorn in every way and for some reason Aquarians seem so attractive in the beginning. They're full of life, light and adventure. Then their real personalities come out. They're distant, cold, controlling and insecure. They don't seem to be able to accept that not everyone thinks and acts exactly like them.

My last girlfriend started the relationship by telling me all about her (ideal) self. She was all about her man, never made a serious decision without consulting him first, loved spending time with me. Then she started to withdraw and became just plain mean. She once told me that I never smiled. I calmly explained to her that I did smile. I just wasn't smiling right now because I had nothing to smile about especially since she was nagging me about not smiling. She was so insecure that she couldn't be wrong about anything.

She once made a statement which was not only not true but so wrong it was actually funny. When I pointed this out she got very upset and insisted that what she said, although physically impossible, was correct. I was having a good time so I just let it go. It really wasn't a big deal. Of course she couldn't and just kept going on about it. I was finally so irritated with her, and that she had pretty much ruined the nice moment we were having, that I proved to her she was wrong.

Her only response was, "Well, it's not like I was that wrong."

I almost walked away right there. What is it about these people that make them need to control everything when they don't even know what's going on half the time? Granted she had some other things going on as well but my experiences with other Aquarians are very similar. I wish there was some way to tell before they get too close."

Here we have the classic air sign/earth sign dilemma. The Capricorn man was being corrected by the Aquarius lady. She obviously has lots of ideas that were very valuable to her. (See my book *How to Bond with an Aquarius*.) Mister Capricorn isn't interested in ideas, unless of course they are going to make a practical difference to his life.

They fell out about an idea, which will crucify an Aquarius and bore the pants off a Capricorn.

He wanted: "life, light and adventure," and ended up with an argument because she couldn't understand that what she had said was physically impossible.

Now another Aquarius wouldn't even *care* about the physical, because they live in ideas land. Mister Capricorn lives in the physical world. This was his undoing.

You can't eat an idea. You can't walk on an idea. You can't drive an idea around the block, or swim with it, or pay it, or put it in your pocket, or sit on it or have it round for tea. You can't make love to an idea or dress it in nice clothes, or admire it or show it to your friends.

Your Capricorn lover will want to immerse himself in the physical world, so make sure you actually like living in and experiencing the physical things before you even attempt a relationship with them.

They were coming from two separate planets. Capricorn is ruled by Saturn, the planet that takes over 28 years to complete its orbit and does so in a steady manner.

Aquarius is ruled by Uranus, the wacky planet that was discovered in Bath where I live. Its orbit is erratic and takes approximately 84 years to work its way through the Zodiac.

So their two astrological rulers were completely different and the only way for them to be united would be for each of them to imagine that they were 'steadily-erratic' or 'erratically-steady'.

Your (female) Capricorn Lover

To understand and appreciate your Capricorn lover I will include a real-life example.

Giselle is an administrator of a large hospital department in London. She organises and implements information from the board of trustees and overseas the general running of various departments. She is divorced and happily single, at the moment, but would love to be in a new relationship (for all the reasons we've discussed in Chapter 1).

Gemini Ascendant, Sun in the 8th, Moon in Taurus

"I'm happy when I'm passionate about something like tango, Qabalah, being in love. Life is enhanced and magical and the senses alive. Everything seems brighter and joyful.

I love beauty in many things, in nature, animals, clothes, jewelry, people outward and inner.

Being in tune with another, whether friend, lover, group.

When I have a deep meditation and feel that sense of stillness, connectedness and peace. I feel and hear a special frequency.

I love it when everything flows at work, home, relationships. There is a sense of harmony.

I love the intimacy with someone special and an exquisiteness of feeling.

I love unique, special and interesting people.

When I've been able to clarify something to someone and get the feedback.

I'm happy when I'm not answerable to anyone and can do exactly what I want."

As you will see from this short excerpt, Giselle is articulate, educated and looking for something to make her 'senses come alive'. She's not looking for ideas. She's looking for feelings, stillness and intimacy. With her Gemini Ascendant, she will want to communicate, with her Sun in the eighth that's where the intimacy comes in and with her Moon in Taurus (which is ruled by Venus) she loves beauty.

To be attractive to and be part of a Capricorn woman's world, you will need to be strong. This is not the same as being bossy, or bullish. You will need strength of character. You will also need to be focused on a future goal, as Capricorns love to be working towards something, rather than reminiscing or wallowing in the now. Keep Mrs. Obama in mind.

I like to ask people in real relationships what their views are about the people in their lives and I asked Barry, who is a musician and sound recordist, (and a Cancer) what would cheer his Capricorn wife up. Here is his reply:

"Money
Security
Judge them at your peril
Remind them how beautiful they are
Remind them how talented they are
Remind them that their worth goes beyond financial reward
Persuade them to go out and have fun
Persuade them to do those things they've been 'meaning to do'
Give them a drink
And another

Allow them not to drink when they don't want
Tear them away from their books occasionally
Encourage them to voice their concerns
Listen to those concerns
But don't judge"

Now if I'm making this sound as if you will have to be next president of the United States of America to hope to date a Capricorn lady, obviously this would be an exaggeration. You will need, though, to grasp the concept of Saturn and all his guises. Don't rush this lady. Remember your manners. Be polite and considerate and save the jolly and frivolous moments for when you know each other better.

What to do when your Capricorn relationship has ended

This is not as difficult as it might be for other star signs. If you're clear, and know what you want, all you have to do is to be completely straight and to the point. Don't dilly-dally. Don't make excuses. Don't get confused or be confusing. Discuss who is going to have what, and make your exit rapid and clear.

If you are on the receiving end of being dumped – sorry, should have said "a relationship ending" – here are a few tips to make yourself feel better.

Fire Sign

If you are a Fire sign – Aries, Leo or Sagittarius – you will need something active and exciting to help you get over your relationship ending.

You will also need to use the element of fire in your healing process.

Get a nice night light candle and light it and recite:

"I… (your name) do let you… (Capricorn's name) go, in the freedom and with love so that I am free to attract my true soul–love."

Leave the night light in a safe place to completely burn away. Allow at least an hour. In the meantime gather up any belongings or possessions that are your now ex-lover's and deliver them back to your Capricorn. It's polite to telephone first and notify your ex when you will be arriving.

If you have any photos of you together or other mementos or even gifts don't be in a rush to destroy them, as some Fire signs are prone to do. Better to put them away in a box in the attic or garage until you feel a little less upset.

In a few months' time go through the box and keep the things you like and give away the things you don't.

Earth Sign

If you are an Earth sign – Taurus, Virgo or our good friend Capricorn – you will feel less inclined to do something dramatic or outrageous. You will also feel as if some part of you has been lost as you are from the same element. It might also take you slightly longer to recover your equilibrium, so allow yourself a few weeks and a maximum of three months to grieve.

You will be using the earth element to help your healing with the use of some trusty crystals.

The best crystals to use are other ones associated with your Sun sign and also with protection.

Taurus = Emerald

Virgo = Agate

If you are a Capricorn yourself you will need Onyx

Cleanse your crystal in fresh running water. Wrap it in some pretty silk fabric, then go on a walk into the countryside. When you find a suitable spot, that is quiet and where you won't be disturbed, dig a small hole and place your crystal in the ground.

Spend a few minutes thinking about your relationship, the good times and the bad. Forgive yourself for any mistakes you may have made.

Imagine a beautiful plant growing from the ground where you have buried your crystal, and the plant blossoming and growing strong.

This will represent your new love that will be with you when the time is right.

Air Sign

If you're an Air sign – Gemini, Libra or Aquarius – you might want to talk about what happened first before you finish the relationship. Air signs need reasons and answers, and can waste precious life-energy looking for those answers. You might need to meet with your Capricorn to tell him/her exactly what you think/thought about his/her opinions, ideas and thoughts. You might also be tempted to tell him/her what you think about them now, which I do not recommend.

Far better to put those thoughts into a tangible form by writing your ex-Capricorn a letter.

It is not a letter that you are actually going to post, but you are going to put as much energy into writing it as if you were actually going to send it.

Write to them thus:

Dear Capricorn,
I expect you will be happy now in your new life, but there are a few things I would like you to know and understand before I say goodbye.

Then list all the annoying, aggravating, upsetting ideas that your now (ex) Capricorn indulged in. Make a list as long as you like. Put in as much detail as you feel comfortable with, including things like how many times they didn't respect your views, or were grumpy with your best friends, or didn't return your calls.

Keep writing till you can write no more, then end your letter with something similar:

"Even though we were not suited, and I suffered because of this, I wish you well on your path," or some other positive comment.

Then tear your letter into teeny little pieces and put them into a small container. We are now going to use the element of air to rectify the situation.

Take a trip to somewhere windy and high, like the top of the hill, and when you're ready open your container and sprinkle a few random pieces of your letter into the wind. Don't use all of the letter or you run the risk of littering, just enough pieces to be significant.

Watch those little pieces of paper fly into the distance and imagine them connecting with the nature spirits.

Your relationship has now ended.

Water Sign

If you are a water sign – Cancer, Scorpio or Pisces – you might find it more difficult to recover quickly from your relationship. You might find yourself weeping at inopportune moments, or when you hear 'Your Song' on the radio, or when you see other couples happily being in each other's company. You might lie awake at night worrying that you have ruined your life and your ex-Capricorn is having all the fun. As you might have gathered by now, this is unlikely. Your ex might be as upset as you.

Your emotional healing therefore needs to incorporate the water element.

As you are capable of weeping for England, the next time you are in floods of tears capture one small teardrop and place it into a small glass. Have one handy just for this purpose. Decorate it if you feel like it. Small flowers, stars, or twinkly things.

Now fill your glass to the top with tap water and place it on a table.

Then recite the following:

This loving relationship with you... (Capricorn name) has ended.

I reach out across time and space to you.

My tears will wash away the hurt I feel.

I release you from my heart, mind and soul.

We part in peace.

And then slowly drink the water. Imagine your hurt dissolving away, freeing you from all anxieties and releasing you from sadness.

Then spend the next few weeks being nice to yourself. If you need to talk, find someone you trust and confide in them. Keep tissues handy.

Your (female) Capricorn Friend

Capricorns make great friends and are very funny to be with, when one is down they are a great pick me up. I found also they make good listeners to helping with other people's problems.

Ex-wife and stepmother to two Capricorns.

Here's Rachel again, we met her in the Intro. Here she is describing the things that make her happy.

Cancer Asc, Sun in 6th, Moon in Aries

"How do I know when I'm happy... I feel content in my body, relaxed and alert and fresh in my mind, interested, excited, open to people and situations. Things are good in my relationships.

I have time for much more and I make time for people. I phone my family more and I enjoy seeing my in-laws and extended family. I'm more tolerant and enjoy people's company. Even if they're not my kind of people, I can like them and value them anyway. I smile at strangers.

I have more to contribute. I can take on more responsibility because it's a breeze. I can invest loads of energy and there is always more available. I have better time management without even noticing. (I hesitate to say that because it sounds 'organised' – to me not having to be organised at all because things fall into place perfectly is more of a virtue than being deliberately organised.)

I am willing to travel. Eager even. Stars and universe seem like a blanket, not a black hole!

My soul is on the same wavelength too (even if on a high octave!). I feel connected. I am overjoyed by serendipity. I always seem to be in the right place at the right time – for myself and others who I encounter at that point. I am enthusiastic about the perfect timing of everything. My goodness if that had happened any earlier it would've been too soon because... such and such... Or people say thanks so much for that (piece of info or thing you just said)... you'll never know why it's made all the difference... and rather than feeling nosy I feel content not to know!

When I'm less happy I retreat from the world for a day or two to recharge my batteries and restore my faith. I feel less inclined to reach out or go the distance. Or I'm out there, coping fine, but less content and less open to new experience because I'm kind of tired with enough already. Or I'm languid but less proactive. Not slug-like necessarily. Perhaps I have more goals. It's as if I notice every-thing isn't perfect. More lists because I have to remember to do things and it's harder to prioritise. I'm less in the flow. I get less happy when loss or confrontation is an issue."

Here we have a few ideas of things:

a) that makes a Capricorn happy and
b) also what qualities you'd need to have, to be a friend to a Capricorn female.

First off, you'd need to be quite independent yourself. There's no mention here of needing to share girly experiences, or wanting to go shopping or chatting. You'll find your Capricorn friend will actually feel happier doing something with you. Doing something responsible, and important. Most, but not all of the Capricorn females I know, have found their friends through work-based activities, as opposed to recreational ones. So to be a Capricorn friend you must have something in common, that you can feel responsible for. And this friendship will last a long, long time.

If you're a flighty Gemini, you might find the prospect of working with someone in a friendship too much like hard work. Your Capricorn friend will want a reason for being friends with you. This is completely different to Aquarian friendships, which just happen. Capricorn friendships are built around work/family/ responsibilities/schools/committees. They are not built on what I call 'fluffiness'. You will be friends because of religion/work/ politics/close proximity. As we learned earlier if you live next door to a Capricorn they are more likely to get to know you, especially more likely to help you, if you're perceived to be needing help, or are 'worse off'. This isn't because of sympathy or power complexes; this is solely because a Capricorn will understand practical needs.

What makes Capricorn friendships more difficult is when there *is* no family and/or no work.

Your (male) Capricorn Friend

Your male Capricorn friend will become so for the same reasons as a female Capricorn. It's just that the environment will be a bit different. Where women are more likely to make friends at the school gates, men will be working together. Obviously with equal rights these things will change but overall most men meet at work or through sport.

Here we have James again. Here he is discussing what it feels like for him to have a Pisces Ascendant. Not every Capricorn will feel like this and I'm including it here to demonstrate how various different aspects of a chart will manifest.

If we were to use a few keywords to describe his chart they would be as follows:

Pisces Ascendant = Sensitive
Sun in the 10th = Focused on career/others' opinions
Moon in Virgo = Good at worrying

You will see this play out as you read through this short excerpt.

James, Pisces Asc, Sun in the 10th, Moon Virgo

"Obviously I can only speak for myself and not for all men, which is probably what you want. Also sensitivity is subjective – I don't know how sensitive others are to measure against. Is there a scale?

I think I am very sensitive. I am affected by criticism and take on insults easily rather than have the ability to shrug them off. Insults often have more weight in my mind than praise. I also think I am quite empathic, although am known to be well off the mark and maybe guilty of projecting my emotions onto others inaccurately.

I think I am more ruled by my emotions than most men, or am not able to bluff it out. I tend to hide in silence or withdraw from difficult emotional situations. From an early age men are encouraged to not show their emotions or let their emotions rule their lives (boys don't cry etc) which is perpetuated in the school playground and cemented in adult life until it is hard-wired .

As demonstrated in the lyrics by a band called James that I always felt rang true:

"Old wives, mystics, hearsay,

wise men, rich men, shaman and sage,

when you're meek on the earth, when you die you will pay,

for accepting that lot, in cheapest of graves.

The sexes divided, men mustn't be weak,
Sensitivity a vice of which we shan't speak."

I think this can be a negative force, leading to frustration and destructive anger, however, seems also to be perpetuated in all media and appears to be attractive to the opposite sex, as the image portrayed is one of men being solid and in control and able to deal with difficult emotional situations without being overwhelmed by them.

Even I feel awkward when I experience men being particularly emotionally demonstrative and am tempted to shrug these situations off with a joke. Although I also admire and empathise with the need to show emotions.

I do feel things but can keep a veneer of passivity, as this seems to be what is expected of me, especially being male, and I can do this very effectively, so much so that when I admit to my feelings to others, they are quite surprised (especially when I have been having a difficult time and I haven't let it show).

I think I have learned to admit to, express and discuss my emotions with close friends, but sometimes I can go too far and admit to feelings and thoughts that maybe I shouldn't. Some things, it appears, should always remain private or hidden.

I can shed a tear at something as simple as a few words heard in a poem or on the radio, or a film or even when reading. This is more likely to happen when I am tired or slightly drunk or particularly inward looking and sensitive.

I was raised in a predominantly female household (father often being absent through work,) and of course I am creative, which means I embark on plenty of introspection, which I think makes me more in touch with my emotions. But I get confused by expectations of male behaviour.

So I guess what this all boils down to is: I think I'm sensitive but feel that I am not allowed to show my emotions."

James is expressing (without any knowledge of Astrology) key parts of his chart. In Astrology anyone can have any Ascendant, Sun or Moon sign, and there is nothing that is especially male or female. That's our take on things, not Astrology's. But you can see here how he struggles with being sensitive, being emotional *and* male. Would it be any different if he were female? And part of that struggle is perpetuated by him having Moon in Virgo, a sign that will deeply analyse things.

Your Capricorn Mother

Your Capricorn mother will be practical. There is no avoiding this. If you are not a practical type yourself you might kick against the idea, especially when you get to your teens, as being a teen is all about rebellion. If you can have an understanding of all the aspects we discussed earlier – the seriousness, responsibility and stoicism – you might feel a little empathy for your Capricorn mother. You might also appreciate the great lengths she will go to, to ensure your life is as trouble-free as possible. However, her determination and focus might drive you crazy.

I was chatting with my osteopath last week. He is in his 40's and his mother is in her 80's. He'd popped round to see her on his way to work (as he is a mum-loving Cancer), and she started having a go at him, because he was wearing cotton trousers. As it was an autumn day and the weather was slightly cooler, she couldn't understand why he wasn't wearing wool trousers… And then spent 20 minutes giving him a: 'you-should-be-wearing-warmer-trousers-for-this-cold-weather' lecture. He launched into: 'I can't wear wool, I work in a warm environment and I'll boil!' But she wasn't going to be corrected. The weather was cold, he should dress warmly.

He beat a hasty retreat!

So let's talk to a real Capricorn mother and find out what happens in her life.

Leo Asc, Sun in 5th, Moon in Virgo

Here we have Olivia, a mum to 6 children, a psychotherapist and Family Constellation Therapist:

"I love classical music and old things, the things I grew up with, I am very sentimental about the old days, old things, old houses, old furniture, small prized possessions from over the years, I can't throw anything out! I love reading and a wide variety of books, I absolutely adore and feel close to or admiring of all animals you could name. I will even talk to a spider and I rescue worms and all creatures that look lost. Always been passionate about horses, and have always had cats, dogs, chickens (not now though) and would have a menagerie. My Mum and Dad were always absolutely the same (he Taurus, she Virgo). Animals are so important in my life. I adore eating vegetables and really chewy bread and old tough cheese! I would not eat chicken or any creature if I had to kill it myself, I just couldn't do this, but I do like eating chicken and salmon and some other fish but not bony or smoked fish. I love the sea and the sands and used to go fishing with the men in a little motorboat when I was a teenager, every summer holiday. I love water anywhere, and countryside though I am not a walker as such. I was always more active, riding, playing tennis, swimming, badminton, table tennis.

I daren't try to play too actively now in case my tendons go, but I also got into an adult learning situation after my first husband died and at the age of 47 went back to college and still love learning stuff. I am not quick at learning but I understand more than I realise, and I have learned that although I don't take in knowledge in an intellectual way, I take things in instinctively and know a lot that I am able to feel I have a good memory now!

That's enough; as you can see, once I get going I say too much probably, but family are very, very important to me indeed."

Now, I didn't ask this Olivia if she found her family important, this was volunteered information and pay attention to it if you want to get on well with your Capricorn mother.

"Family are very, very important to me indeed."

Now, she could have said: "My family are important to me," i.e. a sense of ownership, or she could have said, "The Family," as an institution, but No, she said, "Family," like you might say, "Breathing."

So, if your upset Capricorn has got a family 'issue' make sure you sort that out first before you even try any cheering-up tactics. And what I loved about this example was her job title: a family constellation therapist. If that isn't a fantastic Capricorn occupation, I don't know what is!

And 'Family' consists of Mum, Dad and the children... after a time, that will evolve into in-laws but only if they are as devoted to the family as the Capricorn is.

My (Paternal) grandmother who I mentioned in the introduction was very hot on family.

She had Moon in Gemini and enjoyed short journeys and chatting about the family to my Mum:

*"...telling me in great detail of her pet hates: all her daughters in-laws, though she adored her son-in-law Alex with whom she could find no fault, but as for **his** parents and brother and sister they received her full disapproval... I soon learnt that when she had got it all off her chest, she soon settled down."*

This doesn't extend to cousins, or Aunties (No!!! Auntie's are SO important in my life... sigh) or what I call sideways relatives. It has to be direct relatives, so your Capricorn will also have a deep interest in great-great-great grandparents and things-that-have-been-handed-down.

Your Capricorn Father
I do know a few Capricorn fathers. They take their families very

seriously. They take their role of provider and leader equally seriously. They also get dreadfully upset if their children get into trouble, or aren't realising their ambitions. Like all the advice I have given you in this little book, please keep in mind what sign you are. If you understand yourself, and your own motivations, you're less likely to clash with other people.

I have heard clients of mine complain about their Capricorn father, if they are Fire signs or Air signs and sometimes Dad is accused of being severe and overly formal.

These tend to be clients whose parents are now very elderly, so maybe this is because of the values of the older generation not fitting in with modern life.

However, I don't have many clients that make an appointment to discuss their father. It might come up in conversation but that isn't the reason they come to see me.

To understand your Capricorn father read back over Chapters 3, 4 and 5 and tackle him based on what element is predominant in his chart.

If he is a Firey Capricorn, you will bond best by doing physical things, being excited, rushing around, being sporty or challenging.

If he is an Airy Capricorn things will need to be discussed, debated, thrashed out, thought about, spoken about and decided.

If he is a Watery Capricorn, he will want to talk about his feelings, other people's feelings, old hurts, old upsetment, sentimental things, things that are cherished.

If he is an Earthy Capricorn he will want to know you have sorted out your physical world. He will be focused on money, security, meals, shopping (food), health, your work, his work, other family members' work and will probably lend you money if you ask nicely!

He's also likely to allow you a considerable amount of responsibility from an early age.

I know a Capricorn father who allowed his young daughter aged five to walk to school on her own. Her journey involved crossing three roads, not especially busy roads but with a regular amount of traffic during the rush hour. I found out later that both she and he were Capricorn.

At the time I was walking my young son to school and noticed her walking unaccompanied.

I visited the family and expressed my worries about her walking on her own, and Dad launched into a vicious tirade. He said if he were too namby-pamby she'd never learn anything, and she needed to learn how to walk on her own. I agreed but pointed out that a child that young might be capable but the risk was with *other* people.

The next time I saw them he was walking her to school, mug of tea in his hand looking very grumpy, as if his breakfast had been disturbed, and her looking equally upset.

Had I known at the time that they were both Capricorn, I would have kept my own opinion!

Your Capricorn Sibling

As I mentioned earlier, my youngest sister is a Capricorn. I now know from having researched this book, spending hours writing and thinking about this sign, that they certainly are happiest when the practical issues of life are sorted. As sisters, we have a very good relationship. I am a water-sign Pisces and we get on well as she has a Pisces Ascendant and I'm a Pisces. We even shared a bedroom when we were younger.

For you to get on well with your Capricorn sibling it does depend on what element you are and also on your Ascendant sign.

For instance if you are a Scorpio with a Sagittarius Ascendant and Moon in Aries, you are unlikely to get on with your Capricorn sibling if they have a Virgo Ascendant and Moon in Cancer. This is where having your complete birth chart is important for true understanding. And sometimes it's hard for a Sun sign astrologer to justify making sweeping statements like Scorpio and Capricorn get on if the above applies.

So let's imagine we are discussing only from the Sun sign perspective, so we can have some common ground.

Generally speaking Capricorns enjoy the family unit. And as we found out earlier that the family unit is important to them.

Here is Mahsuri, an alternative health practitioner who has Moon in Gemini talking about what makes her happy:

"Happiness for me is having a sense of feeling at ease within myself and the world, and fully participating in all that life has to offer. Being happy is also being in the company of dear family and friends, having people to share your life with.

I know I am happy when my relationship with my immediate family and the world at large is effortless, that does not occupy unnecessary mental space or is all-consuming and I am in the moment of just being, appreciating the beauty and creativity that is all around me."

She wants her immediate family (not distant relatives) to *not* take up all her mental space. What she means is she doesn't want to have to *think* about her family, just to be part of it.

Too much discussion about things will drive your Capricorn to distraction.

If you are an Air sign you will want things to be debated, discussed and to clear the air. This is not Capricorn territory. The expectation is for everyone to do what they're supposed to do and just get on with it.

I know a family where one sibling is Capricorn and the other is Gemini. Over the years this has caused them an enormous amount of misunderstanding. The Gemini wants to discuss and get straight XYZ, while the Capricorn either does or doesn't want to do certain things. End of. No amount of discussion or persuading will get the Capricorn to do things they don't want to do, while the Gemini thinks things can be resolved by talking about them.

They might resolve things if they respect each other's viewpoint. The Gemini wants certain things to be agreed, verbally. The Capricorn wants to see some action, some tangible results before making a choice. They also should be allowed to say no, and for that 'no' to be respected. Because in their mind if you ask someone if they want to do something and they reply no, they're just being honest!

I hope you have enjoyed learning a little about Astrology and a little about the Sun sign Capricorn. I hope this helps you understand our winter born sign of the Zodiac a bit more.

If you need more information please look in the reference section or my website www.maryenglish.com.

I am writing this in my front room office, in Bath the World Heritage site in the West of England. I am a Pisces. I am happy in my job, with my husband, with my son and with my family. I know that life can be made from good or bad and I decided, not so long ago, to focus on the good.

If we all understood each other a little more, then maybe we could get on a bit better.

There is a candle burning by me and I know that this flame is stronger than discontentment and discord.

I wish you all the peace in the world... and happiness too.

Further Information

www.astro.com – Enormous Swiss website with a lot of free information and a good forum used by astrologers.

www.astrologicalassociation.com – Website of The Astrological Association of Great Britain, a good UK membership organization.

www.bachcentre.com – Home of Dr. Edward Bach and the Bach flower remedy system.

www.astro.com/astro-databank/Main_Page – Astro-Databank: Great website that holds birth data of famous people.

www.astrotheme.com – Privately owned French website with a great search facility for birth data.

Bibliography

1. and 13. *The Dawn of Astrology, Volume 1: The Ancient and Classical Worlds*, Nicholas Campion, 2008, Continuum Books, 11 York Road, London, SE1 7NX, www.continuumbooks.com

2. *The Astrologers and Their Creed, An Historical Outline*, Christopher McIntosh, 1971, Arrow Books Ltd, 3 Fitzroy Square, London W1.

3. *The New Waite's Compendium of Natal Astrology*, Colin Evans, edited by Brian E.F. Gardener, 1967, Routledge and Kegan Paul Ltd, London, UK.

4. *How to Write an Astrological Synthesis*, Terry Dwyer, 1985, LN Fowler Ltd, Romford, Essex, UK.

5. *Picking Your Perfect Partner Through Astrology*, Mary Coleman, 1996, CRCS Publications, USA.

6. *Linda Goodman's Sun Signs*, 1976, Pan Books Ltd, London SW10.

7. *Easy Astrology Guide, How to Read Your Horoscope*, Maritha Pottenger, 1991, ACS Publications, CA, USA.

8. *How to Read Your Astrological Chart, Aspects of the Cosmic Puzzle*, Donna Cunningham, 1999, Samuel Weiser, York Beach ME, USA.

9. *The Only Way to Learn Astrology, Basic Principles*, Marion D. March & Joan McEvers, 1981, ACS Publications.

10. http://theweald.org/N10.asp?NId=1309
11. *Winnie-The-Pooh*, A.A. Milne, 1969, Methuen & Co Ltd,

London EC4.

12. http://en.wikipedia.org/wiki/Elvis_Presley

13. See above

14. Rodden Rating, named after Lois M. Rodden who collected birth data and rated it from A–D depending on how reliable the information is.

http://www.astro.com/astro-databank/Help:RR

References

Dido, 25-12-1971, London, no birth time, Moon Aries

Michele Obama, 17-01-1964, Chicago, IL, USA, no birth time, Moon Aquarius

Kate Moss, 16-01-1974, Croydon, UK, no birth time, Moon Scorpio

Nigella Lawson, 6-01-1960, London, no birth time, Moon Aries

Heather Mills, 12-01-1968, Aldershot, UK, Moon Gemini

A.A. Milne, 18-1-1882, Kilburn, London, no birth time, UK, Moon Capricorn

Rowan Atkinson, 6-1-1955, County Durham, UK, no birth time, Moon Gemini

Mother Meera, 26-12-1960, 6am, Chandepalle, India. Ascendant Sagittarius, Sun 1st, Moon Aries.

Patti Smith, 30-12-1946, Chicago, IL, USA, 6:01am, Ascendant Sagittarius, Sun 1st, Moon Pisces

Elvis Presley, 8-1-1935, Tupelo, MS, USA, 4:35am, Ascendant Sagittarius, Sun 2nd, Moon Pisces

Marcia Starck, 24-12-1939, 2:38am, Patterson, NJ, USA, Ascendant Scorpio, Sun 2nd, Moon Gemini

Isaac Newton, 4-1-1643, 1:38am, Woolsthorpe, UK, Ascendant Libra, Sun 3rd, Moon Cancer

Edgar Allan Poe, 19-1-1809, 1am, Boston, MA, USA, Ascendant Scorpio, Sun 3rd, Moon Pisces

Howard Hughes, 24-12-1905, Houston, Texas, USA, Virgo Ascendant, Sun 4th, Moon Sagittarius.

Rudyard Kipling, 30-12-1865, 10pm, Bombay, India, Virgo Ascendant, Sun 4th, Moon Gemini.

Annie Lennox, 25-12-1954, 11:10pm, Aberdeen, Scotland, Virgo Ascendant, Sun 4th, Moon Capricorn.

Rod Stewart, 10-1-1945, 1:17am, Highgate, London, Libra Ascendant, Sun 4th, Moon Scorpio.

Tracey Ullman, 30-12-1959, 3:15am, Burnham, England, Scorpio Ascendant, Sun in 2nd, Moon in Capricorn.

J.R.R. Tolkien, 3-1-1892, Bloemfontein, South Africa, 10pm, Virgo Ascendant, Sun 5th, Moon Pisces

Dolly Parton, 19-1-1946, Louise Ridge, TN, USA, 8.25pm, Virgo Ascendant, Sun 5th, Moon Virgo

Dennis Wheatley, 8-1-1897, London, England, 7:30pm, Leo Ascendant, Sun 5th, Moon Pisces.

Cynthia Payne, 24-12-1931, Bognor Regis, England, 9pm, Leo Ascendant, Sun 5th, Moon Scorpio.

Muhammad Ali, 17-1-1942, Louisville KY, USA, 6:35pm, Ascendant Leo, Sun 6th, Moon Aquarius

Crystal Gayle, 9-1-1951, Paintsville KY, USA, 1:25am, Ascendant Libra, Sun 3rd, Moon Aquarius.

Kate Bosworth, 2-1-1983, Van Nuys, CA, USA, 5:55pm, Cancer Ascendant, Sun 6th, Moon Virgo.

Ricky Martin, 24-12-1971, Hato Rey, Puerto Rico, USA, 5pm, Ascendant Gemini, Sun 7th, Moon Pisces

Noel Tyl, 31-12-1936, 3:57pm, West Chester, PA, USA, Ascendant Cancer, Sun 7th, Moon Leo.

Jack London, 12-1-1876, San Francisco, CA, USA, 2pm, Ascendant Gemini, Sun 8th, Moon Leo.

Marianne Faithfull, 29-12-1946, London, England, 12:30pm, Ascendant Taurus, Sun 9th, Moon Pisces

Joan Baez, 9-1-1941, Staten Island, NY, USA, 10:45am, Ascendant Aries, Sun 10th, Moon Gemini.

Donna Rice, 7-1-1958, New Orleans, LA, USA, 9:17am, Ascendant Aquarius, Sun 11th, Moon Leo.

Benjamin Franklin, 17-1-1706, Boston MA, USA, 10:30am, Ascendant Aries, Sun 10th, Moon Pisces

Odetta Holmes, 31-12-1930, Birmingham Al, USA, 9:30am, Ascendant Aquarius, Sun 11th, Moon Taurus

David Bowie, 8-1-1947, Brixton, London, England, 9:15am, Aquarius Ascendant, Sun 12th, Moon Leo.

Janis Joplin, 19-1-1943, Port Arthur, TX, USA, 9:45am, Ascendant Aquarius, Sun 12th, Moon Cancer.

Mao Tse-Tung, 26-12-1893, Siangtan, China, 7:30am, Ascendant Capricorn, Sun 12th Moon Leo

Kenny Everett, 25-12-1944, Crosby, England, 3:00am, Ascendant Libra, Sun 3rd, Moon Taurus

Nicolas Cage, 7-1-1941, Harbor City, CA, USA, 5:30am, Ascendant Sagittarius, Sun 1st, Moon Libra

Kevin Costner, 18-1-1955, Lynwood CA, 9:40pm, Ascendant Virgo, Sun 5th, Moon Sagittarius

Tiger Woods, 30-12-1975, Long Beach CA, USA, 10:50pm, Ascendant Virgo, Sun 4th, Moon Sagittarius

Sandy Denny, 6-01-1947, Wimbledon, UK, 4pm, Ascendant Cancer, Sun 7th, Moon Cancer

Client X, 14-1-1963, Liverpool, UK, 10:35am, Ascendant Pisces, Sun 10th, Moon Virgo.

Client Y, 19-1-1980, Miami, Florida, 12:29am, Libra Ascendant, Sun 4th, Moon Aquarius

Client Z, 9-1-1965, London, 4pm, Ascendant Cancer, Sun 6th, Moon Aries

Index

97

BOOKS

O is a symbol of the world, of oneness and unity. In different cultures it also means the "eye," symbolizing knowledge and insight. We aim to publish books that are accessible, constructive and that challenge accepted opinion, both that of academia and the "moral majority."

Our books are available in all good English language bookstores worldwide. If you don't see the book on the shelves ask the bookstore to order it for you, quoting the ISBN number and title. Alternatively you can order online (all major online retail sites carry our titles) or contact the distributor in the relevant country, listed on the copyright page.

See our website **www.o-books.net** for a full list of over 500 titles, growing by 100 a year.

And tune in to myspiritradio.com for our book review radio show, hosted by June-Elleni Laine, where you can listen to the authors discussing their books.